Olen

Bless You

RISE ABOVE IT ALL

Hervey L. Chambers

RISE ABOVE IT ALL

INSPIRATIONAL POETRY

By

HERVEY L. CHAMBERS

ISBN: 0-9702998-2-6

Library of Congress Control Number: 2003108475

LEATHERS
PUBLISHING

A division of Squire Publishers, Inc.
4500 College Blvd.
Leawood, KS 66211
1/888/888-7696
www.leatherspublishing.com

DEDICATION

In memory of my soul mate,
Minister Jennifer K. Chambers,
who was a living testimony
that we can, as she did,
"Rise Above It All,"
and who in her physical absence continues
to encourage and inspire me to press toward the mark
of that high calling in Jesus Christ,
to be fully persuaded, totally committed
and always abounding in love.

Jennifer was to bring the Women's Day message on April 9, 2003. This poem was to introduce her to the congregation. She died before sun-up.

First I thank God, then all of you
for inviting us to share.
Allow me to introduce the Woman of God,
a woman of faith and prayer.

She is the wind beneath my wings;
it's because of her I soar.
She's the virtuous woman that's spoken of
that all who have met still adore.

There's a spiritual aura around her;
it's the way she carries herself.
She tries to get all God has to give,
then she gives until there's nothing left.

Both men and women seek her counsel
to talk, to question, to pray.
Somehow they know if it comes from her
she's going to tell it God's way.

She'll be giving to you what thus said the Lord
according to His word.
Follow along if you brought your Bible;
it's written, it's not something she heard.

She's the perfect example of a wife and mother,
a person couldn't have a better friend.
I know you'll be blessed when she shares God's words
and may not want her sermon to end.

She has always allowed me to be the man
in the decisions that I've had to make.
She is always there to encourage and comfort
even when I make mistakes.

For those of you who know her well
and heard her speak in the past,
you already know what you're in for;
she teaches God's word with class

If you've never heard her, you won't soon forget;
today may even change your life.
Ladies and gentlemen, may I introduce
Jennifer Chambers, my lovely wife.

You walked, you fought, now rest.

ACKNOWLEDGMENTS

All praise, honor, glory and thanksgiving to my Lord and Savior Jesus Christ for choosing me, using me to reveal and share His Word through poetic verse.

To my wonderful family, both nuclear and extended, for the joys and sorrows we shared through the years. God has blessed me to reflect, through poetry, some of my life's thought, feelings and experiences of which you are an integral part.

Special thanks to the St. Mark Baptist Church family, friends and relatives, for your warmth and support during a most difficult time in my life, and to my daughter, LaKesha, for her proofreading skills.

In memory of my late wife, Jennifer K. (Smith) Chambers. Thank God for you, the love we shared and for the influence you had on my life. Because of Christ in you, I am who I am.

Hervey L. Chambers

TABLE OF CONTENTS

INTRODUCTION

Why is it that so many people do not accept Christ when He is presented to them?

1. The mind of some people is literally bound by the principalities, dark powers and rulers of this earth.

2. Many people do not recognize the enemy and his tactics, which allows him to infiltrate and destroy many individual lives, homes and churches because they don't know how to combat the unknown. Hosea 4:6, My people perish (are destroyed) for a lack of knowledge.

3. Some people don't realize that when they open the door to their spiritual life (their heart), the enemy comes in, in disguise, and seizes the opportunity to kill and destroy. He seeks the same thing from all people.

4. Many people don't recognize the things that are influencing their lives as tricks of the devil, pride, self gratification, etc.

5. Some people are simply lost. II Corinthians 4:4, the gods of this world have blinded their minds.

In all things that come before us, purge them first, look for the enemy. Close the door of our heart to sin. The fields of our lives have been mined by the enemy and must be defused before they explode. Traps must be located and sprung before we trap ourselves.

We must recognize the openings (doors) created by sin in our lives that makes us vulnerable to the enemy. When we yield to temptation and sin, we are not protected. To continue to live in sin requires our conscious participation. We are servants to obey whomever we choose to be our master, either of sin unto death, or of obedience unto righteousness. Romans 6:15-16

God has set before us life and death, the choice is ours, blessings and curses. We can yield to Satan, sin and self, or we can look to Jesus, the author and finisher of our faith and **Rise Above It All.**

RISE ABOVE IT ALL

Since the time of Adam and Eve in the garden
when Satan made his very first call,
Man has been struggling within himself
trying to rise above it all.
Genesis 3

The wickedness of man was great in the earth,
evil thoughts and imaginations his sort.
It repented the Lord that he had made man,
and it grieved him to his heart.
Genesis 6:5-6

But Noah found Grace in the eyes of the Lord
and was told to make an ark while it's dry;
and of every living thing of all flesh take two,
a coming flood would cause all to die.
Genesis 6:8 -7:5

It was not raining in this desert place
when Noah received the command,
but he followed instructions for 120 years,
as he laid out the blueprints and plan.

You know the story, how they laughed at Noah;
they considered him a fool gone mad.
He continued to build, on faith, with patience;
he understood the awesome task he had.

Just as God promised, the rains began,
and they lasted 40 days and nights.
Can you imagine the people around day 27,
as they now considered their plight.

1

Noah did according as the Lord commanded,
and the ark was three stories tall.
When the waters covered this evil land,
the ark rose above it all.
Genesis 6:16-7:10

Zaccheus was the chief among the Publicans;
he was rich as rich could be.
He sought to see Jesus but he was little of stature,
so he climbed up a Sycamore tree.
Luke 19:1-9

Because of the crowd and because of his size,
Zacchaeus was not very tall;
he really wanted an audience with Jesus
and had to rise above it all.

We are no different and must do what it takes,
and all it really takes is the Word,
Faith, obedience, and a heart full of love,
in response to the voice we heard.

The problem has been trying to do it ourself;
thus we fail because we don't know
that we must be led and guided by the Spirit;
the word of God in our lives must show.
Proverbs 1:22-25
Romans 8:14

It's not good enough to just know the word;
mere knowledge is where we begin.
For a person to know but then not do,
for that person this is a sin.
James 1:23

When we accept Jesus Christ as Lord and Savior;
when we heed his almighty call
by being obedient to his commands,
we can rise above it all.
Joshua 1:8

Despite all the evil in the world today
with values and morals run aground,
trusting in God with enduring faith,
man can turn his situation around.
Mark 11:23

If we who are Christian would humble ourselves,
turn from evil ways and pray,
God promised to heal our sin-sick land,
to be with us he would always stay.
II Chronicles 7:14

Every day of our life will not be easy;
we will stumble and sometimes fall,
but by repenting, with a sincere heart
we can rise above it all.
Psalm 37:23-24

With our corrupt officials and political preachers,
there are some who are one and the same.
School children killing children, babies making babies,
we have only ourselves to blame.
I Corinthians 15:33

Where is the example they are to follow?
We should raise them in the way they should go.
While we're leaving God out of their formative years,
we expect them into Christians to grow.
I Timothy 4:12

Someone has to lay a solid foundation
upon which our children can build.
Christ is that rock, our life's cornerstone,
when we submit to his way and his will.
Psalms 118:22
Matthew 21:42

Many have strayed in this walk of life;
others simply ran from the call,
but Christ said "Stand" on his word, just "Stand,"
and we can rise above it all.
Ephesians 6:13-14

We all have to crawl before we can walk;
we must rise before we can stand.
We can't wallow in the cesspool of sin
and claim to be holding God's hand.

It's Christ carrying us on this life's journey;
it's not the other way around.
It's Christ that chose us to be his people,
but it's we that are letting him down.

Some people seem to think that life is a game
that rolls on and on like a ball.
The word says study to show yourself approved
and learn to rise above it all.
II Timothy 2:15

Examine yourself, do not judge others;
use the Lord Jesus Christ as your measure.
Worry not about what others may say,
know that God looks at you as his treasure.
II Corinthians 13:5
II Corinthians 4:7

God sees us in the spirit realm;
in our heart is where he placed his law.
It's up to us to obey his word
and rise above our human flaw.

It's each person's choice to get their flesh
under subjection and aligned with the word,
To seek for themselves the kingdom of God
and not rely on some doctrine they heard.
Romans 8
Matthew 6:33

All men's hearts are not pure as snow;
they anxiously wait for us to fall,
but by acknowledging God in all our ways,
we can rise above it all.
Proverbs 3:6

God will not bribe or threaten us
to get us to obey.
His commandments are firm, yet he remains loving
and he'll let us do things our way.

Sometimes our behavior will hinder God's work,
at least in the eyes of man,
but have no doubt, no matter what we think,
it's all part of his master plan.

One man's trash is another man's treasure,
I've heard that saying in part.
Christ is the man taking up collection,
and he's waiting at the door to your heart.

No pain, no gain, no guts, no glory,
commitment comes with a cost.
Christ gave his life for the sins of the world;
he paid the cost to be the boss.

From the time he descended from heaven on high
until he finished our Father's call,
He was a living testimony and
He rose above it all.

We think of ourselves as mighty men,
world leaders with status and clout;
we fail to remember from whence we came,
and our future is certainly in doubt.

We all know the best route to follow,
so why aren't we all on the road?
Being a Christian is more than Sunday worship;
it's a lifestyle of love, that's our load.

It's a load we should share that should get lighter
as we give love to all that we meet,
but we can't give something that we don't have;
we need to fall on our face at God's feet.

And now we can only blame ourselves
for the perils that we are in;
we did it our way, apart from God,
we succumbed to temptation and sin.

How did we get so far off track?
Was it because of the party line
when we left Christ out of our daily decisions
we were left with a reprobate mind?

We have heart trouble, our conscience is seared,
we have no respect for life;
the shedding of blood have lost its meaning
as long as it's the poor that sacrifice.
I Timothy 4:1-2
Psalm 51:6-7

Create in us a clean heart, O God,
and renew a right spirit within;
restore to us the joy of salvation
and cleanse us from our sin.
Psalm 51:10-12

Our CEOs and our men at the top
all seem to be above the law;
for filthy lucre they sold out to Satan,
and our country is now seeing their flaw.

Instead of playing by the rules of law,
some players tried to do an end run (ENRON).
The market collapsed, many people were hurt;
now Congress has them under the gun.

Some things are done in ignorance and unbelief,
but we know that the law is good;
man's law is not made for the righteous man
who follows God's law like he should.
I Timothy 1:8-13

From the Highest Seat in our national government
to the lowest at community level,
we have forsaken our God, pushed him aside
and made easy in-roads for the devil.

Car bombings, kidnappings, molesting young children,
there's only one safe place to be:
connected to the vine, rooted and grounded
in the love of God, set free.
John 15:1-8
Ephesians 3:14-19

There are only two forces in all of the world,
and each one of them have a master;
we cannot serve both, we must make a decision
or we head for certain disaster.
Matthew 6:24

When we are lukewarm, God will spew us out;
it's because we have left our first love.
We must repent, we must do the first works
and return to our Lord God above.
Revelations 2:4-5

In all our ways we must acknowledge God;
there are some things a man should not do.
Taking God and prayer out of school was wrong,
a sad chapter for our ACLU.
Proverbs 3:6
Proverbs 6:16-19

We all have sinned and come short of God's Glory;
my appeal is to those in authority.
We must demonstrate love to all of God's people,
not just our own little party.

Liberals, Conservatives, Democrats, Republicans,
all should be brothers in Christ;
not any one of us have all the answers,
so let's do it God's way and be nice.

God places in our path many individuals,
and through them He reveals himself.
We squander opportunities to be His instrument
when we leave His love on a shelf.

Christ in me, the hope of glory,
should be the Christian's battle cry during trial;
God expects us to be obedient
with a living testimony lifestyle.

If God's people which are called by his name
would humble themselves and pray,
turn from wicked ways and seek his face,
He will heal our land someday.
II Chronicles 7:14

We need right now a touch from God
because the world, like a baby, can't rest
when it's longing for the comforting caress of the parent
and the parent is not doing their best.

Michelangelo's painting in the Sistine Chapel
of God extending a hand toward man
or like the woman with the issue of blood,
we must try to touch God, and we can.
Matthew 9:20-23

If two or three are gathered in the name of Jesus
and shall agree as touching when they ask
it will be done by Father God in heaven,
any thing done by him will last.
Matthew 18:19-20

When we say one thing but do another,
what kind of a message is sent?
It's time to start being for real with God,
and the first step is we must repent.

For all the conniving things we've done,
whether in word or in deed,
Father, forgive us, we submit ourselves;
place us in the body as you need.

Fill us with your spirit and bridle our tongue;
teach us patience as we learn to cope.
Bless us with the greatest, the gift of love
as we serve and continually hope.
I Corinthians 13:13

We realize you know the intents of our heart
and we are all well aware of your word,
but we don't understand your concept of love;
we don't study, we go by what's heard.
Hebrew 4:12
II Timothy 2:15

Our salvation began with your loving plan,
the atoning death on the cross of our Lord;
forgiveness and cleansing was through the Holy Spirit,
it's the Trinity some people find so hard.

It confounds their mind but comforts their soul,
each person of the Godhead unique;
help us understand your triune being
as your word we come to know and to speak.

Help us to give you first place in our lives;
our freedom came with a cost.
Keep us mindful of the price your Son had to pay
for the redemption of our souls that were lost.

Father; help us submit to your will and your way
and please pick us up when we fall,
as we press toward the mark of your high calling;
Father, help us to rise above it all.

MISTAKES

Now that the son has risen in your life,
and the two of you started this walk,
you're beginning to **rise above it all;**
let's continue our brotherly talk.

As a man of God and a Deacon in particular,
to tell the truth I am duty bound.
The sermons I preach through poetic verse,
search the scriptures, the doctrine is sound.
II Timothy 4:2

Almost every verse has the scripture listed,
so you can read for yourself.
Don't rely on your pastor, any man, or me,
get your Bible down from the shelf.

People perish for a lack of knowledge,
and Christ wants you to know.
He really wants you to understand
that sound doctrine is the way to go.
Hosea 4:6

People spin the scriptures many ways
to fit their needs or whims.
God said in his word that he would supply,
if we believe, obey and follow him.
Matthew 22:23-30
Hebrews 3:7-15

Of all the people in the Holy Bible,
every one of them had a fault.
Jesus was the only exception;
He lived the life that He taught.
I Peter 2:22   *Luke 23:4*

Even He had a moment of weakness,
or was it a sign of strength?
When He cried for relief of his afflictions,
under pressure for such a great length.
Hebrew 5:7-9   Mark 15:34

Job was a perfect and an upright man;
He never lost faith in the Master.
He endured the hardships and passed his test
in the face of all disaster.
Luke 22:42-45

Abraham journeyed and went into Egypt
and stretched the truth to a guy;
about Sarai his wife, being his sister,
because he did not want to die.
Genesis 12:1-13

Abraham still believed in the Lord,
and the Lord continued to bless.
A covenant was made, some names were changed,
because Abraham had passed the test.
Genesis 15:6-17:15
Romans 4:3

Abraham is known as the Father Of Faith;
through him many nations came.
We're descendants of his through his seed,
his promises are ours to claim.
Genesis 17:19

Moses questioned some of God's instructions
and didn't always do as he was told.
God used his brother as a go-between;
Aaron spoke to the people quite bold.
Exodus 4:1-15

Nevertheless Moses was the leader;
God still kept him in charge
of the exodus from old Pharaoh's control,
and the journey to the land so large.
Exodus 4:16, 29-31   Exodus 13:17-22

David was a man after God's own heart,
but he chose to have another man's wife.
As bad as that was, he went even further
and caused Uriah to lose his life.
I Samuel 13:14
Acts 13:22
II Samuel 11:14-17

He was still the King and had to rule,
even though he committed the sin.
He was God's choice and he was responsible
for the kingdom and all therein.
II Samuel 12:7-14

What David had done displeased the Lord;
He sent Nathan across the land
To relay to David the story of two men.
Nathan said, "Thou art the man."
II Samuel 11 and 12

The Lord put away David's sin
because he repented to God with a cry;
but the sin was committed, a price had to be paid;
the illegitimate son had to die.

Even brother Jonah had some problems,
following the Lord's command
about going to Ninevah to warn the people,
and the other way old Jonah ran.
Jonah Chapter 1-4

He set sail on a ship going the opposite direction
from where God told him to go.
A storm arose, the whole ship was in trouble;
Jonah hid in the deck below.

Jonah was cast into the sea,
where a great fish swallowed him whole.
Jonah prayed unto God, was vomited on the land,
and to Ninevah God's story was told.

According to the word in Jonah chapter three,
the journey was a good three days.
Jonah made it in one, after he paid attention
and changed his disobedient ways.

Many people make a grave mistake
by burying the gifts God gives.
He endows each Christian through the Holy Spirit
to ensure His church will live.
Romans 12:3-8
I Corinthians 12

So many are reluctant to obey the Lord
and struggle to do what is right.
The simple answer is go with God
and walk by faith, not by sight.
Mark 16:15-18
II Corinthians 5:7

Sinful habits can be broken,
as shown by example of these men.
Acknowledge, repent, believe, don't doubt,
be persuaded that with God you will win.
Romans 6:12-14
Romans 10:9-10

Be fully persuaded, totally committed,
that God is more than enough.
His grace is sufficient in any situation,
when the word becomes alive in us.
Ephesians 3:20
Romans 8:38
II Corinthians 12:9

Dying unto self may be one tough job;
but the privilege is beyond all price.
The Lord gives wisdom to those who submit,
who walk and have the mind of Christ.
Proverbs 2:6   James 1:5
I Corinthians 2:16   Philippians 2:5

These men didn't earn their way into heaven,
it's by faith they were justified.
Neither can we live by bread alone,
our God must be glorified.
Romans 3:28   James 2:21-24
Matthew 4:4

Salvation is a gift, it's not a paycheck;
some people will be shocked and amazed
when they finally learn that according to the word,
they must endure to the end to be saved.
Ephesians 2:8
Matthew 24:13   Mark 13:13

In spite of mistakes that we have made,
our Lord God will take us back,
if we repent and live, in obedience and faith;
and run the race on God's holy track.
I John 1:7-10

No person I know is temptation proof;
even mature Christians holy and meek.
Watch and pray lest you enter temptation,
because the human flesh is weak.
Matthew 26:41

A temptation can be most anything,
that's contrary to God's holy will:
Chronic impatience, a critical tongue, the love of money,
or as simple as taking a pill.
I Corinthians 10:3

Do you even know your spiritual weakness,
That area of your unguarded soul?
It may be your failure to ask for God's strength
is the greatest weakness you have as a whole.

Another mistake is trying to do things yourself;
allow God to work through you.
His indwelling presence is all you need
for your days to be rosy and not blue.

VAPOR

Your life's been spent doing as you choose
with no thought of Jesus Christ our Lord,
But now that you're getting on in age,
going to church doesn't seem so hard.

You were running the streets, getting drunk and lying,
committing all kinds of sin.
In the deep waters of life about to drown,
now you call to the Savior "Let Me In."
Noah's Ark

During all those years he was calling you,
you always went the other way.
He was not important, you were in command
and didn't care what He had to say.
Jonah

You didn't serve God while in your youth;
you danced to the tunes of the world.
Now that you can't keep in step,
you need Jesus for this last twirl.
Ecclesiastes 12:1

He know the thoughts and intents of your heart,
so are you serious with him when you say,
"I accept you as Lord and Savior of my life"?
This is not a game you play.
Hebrews 4:12

Even if it was you couldn't win,
he controls your every breath,
and he'll forgive like he did before,
but the wages of sin is death.
Romans 6:23

18

Now that you're old, wrinkled, and grey, and
there's aches all over your body,
You turn to the church, seeking relief,
from a life of mundane melancholy.

You want to sing in the choir, be an usher
or drive the transport van.
The world has kicked you to the curb,
and now you want to be God's man.

Since the God we serve is gender free,
this poem is for women, too.
Some of you women are worse than men;
let him create a clean heart in you.
Psalm 51:10

You can still be of service to God Almighty,
even though you're lame and old.
You're a living example that he'll see you through,
and **His Story** still needs to be told.

Don't rejoice, or boast, brag about your past,
when you know you were living a lie.
Don't let your old age go to your head,
because you really weren't fit to die.

God was giving you time to see his light,
he loves you but hates your sin.
You wanted what was yours like the Prodigal Son,
but now it's time to come on in.

What is your life? It is even a vapor;
it appears for a while, then it's gone;
and since tomorrow is not promised to us,
it's today we must sing Zion's song.
James 4:14-17

THE COLD WITHIN

We say it sure is cold outside,
when the icicles are long and thin.
But no cold can compare to the unsaved man
and the cold he has within.

It's bad enough to be lost and alone;
most unsaved folk need a friend,
Someone to blame when things go wrong,
to keep fueling the cold within.

Each generation get worse and worse;
as teachers, pastors and priests turn to sin.
Having sex with their students and molesting the kids,
putting ice on the cold within.

Our country was founded on religious principles;
our money says "In God We Trust."
The love of this currency is the root of all evil
and is causing man to go bust.

From the **Highest Seat** of political office,
to the homeless person with needs,
The cold within affects every nation,
all races, all colors and all creeds.

How did we get to where we are?
Where do we go from here?
Continue to remove Christ from our midst,
or keep his commandments in fear?

When all else fails, follow instructions;
Christ gave us the **Saving Plan.**
Read and study, ask God to reveal
how to heat the cold within man.

Each child of God is a piece of the puzzle,
if each would answer their call.
The objective, to be fitly joined together,
and **Rise Above It All.**

Those things that divide are things of the devil,
tricks of Satan mere illusions.
God is not causing the cold within;
he is not the author of confusion.

America the Beautiful, home of the free,
a melting pot where liberties stand,
is slowly but surely losing her stature,
succumbing to the cold within man.

Every nation, every sect, every clan, each person;
not one is immune to sin;
but each could provide some relief to the world
by praying; Jesus, heat the cold within.

It's all in the heart; that is where God looks,
that is where his laws abide.
It's up to each person to examine himself
and to lay every weight aside.

Whatever is causing problems in our life,
Jesus is the answer, I know.
He promised to never leave us alone,
if only to him we would go.

He did not say we wouldn't be tempted,
but yield not, for yielding is sin.
Rise above and overcome your situation;
apply Jesus to the cold within.

Thoughts and ideas, actions and deeds
are subject to the person's will.
When left unchecked by the Word of God,
eventually the spirit sits still.

Awaiting for you to repent and submit,
turn your back on the world of sin,
Let Jesus be Jesus in all that you do;
he can warm the cold within.

SIN NO MORE

Woe to them that are at ease,
that trust in the world and its way,
Whose beds of ivory and bowls of wine
are not shared with God's children today.
Amos 6:1-6

All things that are made were made by Him;
for our good everything was meant,
but we over-indulged, greed and pride set in,
and then toward sin we were bent.
John 1:1-3

We can reverse this worldly trend
by doing what the Bible bid.
Believe, repent, live an obedient life,
and remember what our Father did.
Plan of Salvation

He laid the foundations of the earth;
he gave the sun its path.
He placed each star and blanket of clouds,
so don't provoke Him to wrath.
Job 38-39   Genesis 1-2   John 1

He's the one that causes each flower to bloom,
and he casts each flake of snow.
He makes thunder roll and the lightning flash,
and he directs each wind to blow.

All of nature is one big-time band,
conducted by Christ the creator,
Everything working together for good,
on stage in His theater.
Romans 8:28

He causes nature to change its pace
from summer to a winter's chill.
A spring for new life and autumn for harvest,
a time for birth and to kill.
Ecclesiastes 3

And we, my friend, must be reborn;
yet we also must die.
Die unto self so that Christ lives within;
it's up to each person to try.
John 3:3

To press for the mark of God's high calling,
not receive God's grace in vain,
Not love in word or in tongue, but in deed
and in truth, with patience, enduring pain.
II Cor. 6:1
I John 3:18

For he is the way, the truth and the life;
you only come to the Father through Christ.
Take a step of faith for God's gift of salvation;
His only son was our sacrifice.
John 14:6

The choice is yours and yours alone;
no one can decide for you.
You have free will, either life or death;
which master will you serve unto?
Joshua 24:15   Matthew 6:24

Don't put off until tomorrow what you can do today,
and smile, otherwise you may weep.
God sees not only how much you give,
but also how much you keep.

Don't be discouraged if your role seems small;
Zechariah 4:10 let's mention.
The widow's mite or your smallest deed
is better than the greatest intention.
Mark 12:42-44

See, you've been made well, sin no more,
lest a worst thing come upon you .
Don't squander God's grace and waste His riches;
do what he has asked you to do.
John 5:14

Being a servant to others opens the door of their heart;
to hear the gospel of Christ we preach.
Through the life we live people are drawn,
and through them other people we can reach.

Helping spread the gospel to every nation
while we personally may never leave town,
Walk in wisdom toward those that are without;
make a difference during your life's countdown.
Colossians 4:5

For to live is Christ and to die is gain;
at death we began to live
Eternally with God, our Lord and Savior;
and forever to him praises give.
Philippians 1:21

He bid us go and sin no more,
to repent if we should fall.
The devil is seeking, roaring as a lion,
but we can **rise above it all.**

GOD'S RELIABLE WORD

All scripture is given by inspiration of God,
for doctrine, for reproof, for correction,
Is profitable for instruction in righteousness,
but we must maintain the connection.
II Timothy 3:16

That as people of God we may be perfect,
thoroughly furnished unto all good work.
Depending on God's reliable word,
and from Satan and sin we shirk.
II Timothy 3:17

For the word of God is quick and powerful,
and we know it endureth forever.
The Lord will hasten to perform His word;
He promised to leave us, never.
I Peter 1:25   Jeremiah 1:12   Hebrews 13:5

Heaven and earth shall pass away,
but not the word of God,
For it is an incorruptible seed,
living in a human pod.
Matthew 24:35   I Peter 1:23

In the beginning was the word,
by the word all things were made.
The Word is our comfort, healing and strength,
when our mind is on Him stayed.
John 1:1-3   Psalms 107 and 119

His divine providence and our human emotion
are not always on an even keel.
Our experiences in life, in connection with God,
is not based on how we feel.

We must stand fast on the word of God;
We are the branch, the Word is the vine.
If we're fully persuaded and totally committed,
God's Word will work every time.
Romans 8:38-38   Luke 9:62   John 15:1-7

He may not come when you want him to,
or come in the form you think.
His ways are not ours and ours are not his,
but his word will work in a blink.
Matthew 8:8 & 8:13

God's Holy Scriptures empower us;
it's our handwriting on the wall.
Through obedience to God's reliable word,
We can **rise above it all.**

WAY OF LIFE

Christ would have us be as one
and He desires that our hearts be pure.
He plainly set forth in the Holy Scriptures
everything for our minds to be clear.
Matthew 5:8
II Timothy 2:15-16

In our human way we have a limited view
of God, who is in us living.
He has designed for us a way of life,
the foundation of which is giving.
John 13:15   15:13
Luke 6:38

God gave His son; His son gave his life;
He died for the sins of all.
He bore our grief, by His stripes we are healed;
the way of life is to heed His call.
John 3:16   Romans 5:8
Galatians 1:3-4
Isaiah 53:4-5

Denominations and traditions are not the way of life;
both cases have a serious flaw.
God demands sincerity of the heart
for that is where He placed His law.
Jeremiah 31:33

If we really understood who God is
and how we are connected to Him,
We would follow the way of life He designed
and not worry so much about **them.**
John 15:1-6
I John 4:7-8

Them being those who are not of the faith —
unbelievers, of every persuasion.
Those who deny the trinity of God
and denounce Him when they have occasion.
Acts 15:7-9

Jesus is the Way, the Truth, and the Life,
the Savior, the Christ, the Son.
He was in the beginning, He is the Word;
He, God and Holy Spirit are one.
John 1:1, 10:30, 14:6
I John 5:7

The breath of life was breathed into us;
the Lord is the strength of our life.
He is married to us, He is the head
we are to Him as a wife.
Genesis 2:7
Psalms 27:1
Jeremiah 3:14

So teach me thy way of peace, O' Lord,
and make all my pathways plain.
Thy word have I hid in my heart, dear God,
it's your wisdom I endeavor to gain.
Psalms 27:11, 119:11
Judges 18:6

Wisdom is too high for a fool;
the way of life is above to the wise.
I'll look to the hills from which cometh my help,
and I'll press toward the mark, I'll rise.
Proverbs 15:24, 24:7
Psalms 121:1-2
Philippians 3:14

RENEWED

Except a man be born again
the kingdom he cannot see.
Born not of blood, nor will of flesh
nor of man, but Christ in thee.
John 3:3
John 13:1

We must be washed and cleansed from sin,
a clean heart and right spirit renew.
Continue in faith; rooted and grounded,
abide in Christ, for He abides in you.
Psalms 51:2   Psalms 51:10
Colossians 1:23   John 15:4-7

In Him we live, move, and have being,
old things are passed away.
The former conversation, the old man put off,
be renewed in Christ day by day.
Acts 17:28   Ephesians 4:22-24
II Corinthians 5:17

Without faith He's impossible to please,
so we walk by faith, not by sight.
He will reward if we diligently seek
and live an humble and obedient life.
Hebrews 11:6   II Corinthians 5:7
Philippians 2:8

To live is Christ, to die is gain,
by faith Christ dwells in our heart.
We shall be saved if we endure to the end;
that means we must do our part.
Philippians 1:21   Ephesians 3:17
Matthew 24:13   II Corinthians 10:5

Abide in the word for it is our life;
it must come alive in us.
We are called to stand firm on the word of God
and in Him put all our trust.
Ephesians 6:13

A complete life in Christ means full persuasion,
total commitment ... no lies.
Be obedient to Christ for He is our master;
it is through His power we rise.

MARTHA S. WHITE
19 October '54—27 October '01

Eye hath not seen, nor ear heard,
neither have entered into the heart of man
the things which God hath prepared
for them that love Him.
I Corinthians 2:9

He have prepared for us a mansion
on the foundation of His love;
He lived and died for our salvation,
and He waits for us above.
John 14:2-3

He is the way, the truth and the life;
the vine of life is He.
In order "To come unto the Father,
every person must come by me."
John 14:6

The Lord is our light and our salvation;
with Him whom should we fear.
He loves and cares, He'll never forsake.
and right now He holds us dear.
Psalm 27:1

We don't know what the future holds,
but your battle has been won,
You chose to live your life for Christ,
a faithful walk with the Son.
II Chronicles 20:15

The beauty of the Lord is ours to behold,
believe to see the goodness therein.
Sing praises to the Lord, sacrifices of joy;
thank Him for forgiveness of sin.
Psalm 27:4, 6, 13

Cast your cares upon the Lord
and accept His peaceful rest.
Man is appointed once to die;
Earthly living, **it's only a test.**
I Peter 5:7   Hebrews 9:27

INSIDE JOB

The law of God is in our heart;
none of our steps shall slide.
We are led by the Spirit, we are children of God;
It's in His love we abide.
Psalm 37:31
Romans 8:14

His word is hidden in our hearts
that we might not sin against thee.
We desireth truth in the inward parts
and His wisdom to set us free.
Psalm 119:11
Psalm 51:6

Christ dwell in the heart of man by faith
that he be rooted and grounded in love.
God shall supply all our needs by Christ Jesus
who intercedes for us above.
Ephesians 3:17
Philippians 4:19

He grants to us the riches of His glory,
spiritual strength in our inner man.
He was tempted in every point as we are;
He was successful so, yes, we can.
Ephesians 3:16
Hebrews 4:5

If we want Christ to abide within,
we must love Him and keep His word.
We must desire His sincere milk
and not every wind of doctrine we've heard.
John 14:23   I Peter 2:1-2
Ephesians 4:14

That which we heard from the beginning,
that's what we should let abide.
Continue in the Son and in the Father
and simply lay every weight aside.
I John 2:24
Hebrews 12:1

We must examine ourselves and we must study;
We also have to watch and pray.
A Christian's life is a spiritual process;
Change comes by doing things God's way.
II Corinthians 13:5
II Timothy 2:15   Mark 14:38

Let Him do for you what needs to be done,
Understand it's an inside job.
He's on the work site, let Him get busy
before the thief comes to steal, kill and rob.
John 10:10

Each person wants to rise above it all,
but before that event takes place,
our spirit is renewed by an inside job,
the love of God, His mercy and His grace.
II Corinthians 4:16

LOVE MAKES IT RIGHT

While in the midst of trials and tribulations
and a person is determined to fight,
listen to the quiet still voice of God
because His love makes it right.
Psalm 95:7-8

Be angry, yes, but do not sin;
Sometimes it's best to listen,
especially when dealing with an unsaved person
and your disagreement thickens.
Ephesians 4:26

This is what Christ Jesus did
when they took Him in the night —
not like Peter who drew his sword
and prepared for a valiant fight.
John 18:10

If you're caught up in a bad situation
and you're misused day and night,
don't worry about what man says or does;
God's love will make it right.

Love your neighbor as you love yourself
and desire for them the best;
Show them love like Christ does for you;
He will add unto you the rest.
Matthew 22:39
Matthew 6:33

So great was the love Christ had for us
that He chose his own life to lay down.
Greater love hath no man than this,
and in God is where love is found.
John 15:13
I John 4:8

Love is the fulfilling of the law,
and sometime things do get tight,
but God makes a way out of what looks impossible;
Always His love makes it right.
Romans 13:10

COURTS OF PRAISE

Each and every day with Jesus
should be deeper than the day before
as we mature in Christ and dedication to God,
giving thanks, praise, worship and adore.

As we consecrate ourselves to Him,
magnify, revere, and give praise,
extolling Him in the highest terms
is how we should start our days.

Bring into intimacy reverent honor to God,
special praise, admiration and devotion,
acknowledgment of His divine favor and love
and not just going through the motion.

From a grateful heart to an awesome God,
honor Him with a submitted life style
because He loved us before we loved Him;
Let's do things His way for a while.

Make a joyful noise unto the Lord,
enter into His courts with praise.
Know that He's God, serve Him with gladness,
acknowledge Him in all thy ways.
Psalm 100
Proverbs 3:6

His gate is the opening or avenue;
It's the channel, the door to our heart.
His courts are the places where God meets us
as we go about doing our part.

He will meet us at the courts of *repentance,*
obedience, instruction and *fear,*
trial, tribulation, weakness, fellowship
and where *suffering* and *death* seem near.

In the Garden of Eden during the cool of the day,
God met with Adam and Eve.
All was well in the court of instruction
until the two of them were deceived.
Genesis Chapter 3

The court of obedience is where Abram met God
as he went where he was told to go.
Each place he stopped, he would set up an altar
so that all of his followers would know.
Genesis Chapter 12

Moses was on top of Mount Sinai
in the court of fellowship, face to face.
He received instructions for the children of God
and led them with God's power and grace.
Exodus Chapter 19

God met Elijah in the court of fear
as he slept underneath a tree.
An angel touched him, said, "Arise and eat,"
go forth, there's no need to flee.
I Kings Chapter 19

David was a man after God's own heart,
but still he committed sin.
God met with him at the court of repentance
and allowed King David to win.
Psalms 51

In the fiery furnace for the Hebrew men
in the court of tribulation and trial.
All three were acquitted, set free by God,
they kept the faith and walked away with a smile.
Daniel Chapter 3

There was given to Paul a thorn in the flesh,
but God's grace was sufficient for thee.
He met Paul in the court of weakness
and that's where He heard his plea.
II Corinthians Chapter 12

In the Garden Of Gethsemane
and Mount Calvary for Jesus
in the court of suffering and death,
God met His Son who rose with all power;
He had passed His earthly test.
Luke Chapter 22 and 23

God will meet us in all these courts;
Praise brings God on the scene.
True praise from a repentant heart,
be thankful you are spiritually clean.

THE DEVIL'S DEVICES

The devil takes advantage of what is available;
he's not developed any new ruse.
Read them all, Genesis through Revelations,
as he puts each one to use.

Devices are things for a particular purpose:
a plan, trick, scheme or plot.
They cause our detour, failure or demise
and Satan uses them a lot.

His purpose is to pull us away from Christ
and get us to join his band.
Maybe he forgot we are **Bought With A Price**
and we are safely in Christ Jesus' hand.
I Corinthians 6:20

He has his job that he must do
lest his pitiful imp army will fall;
so he goes to and fro testing his devices,
trying to get us to go AWOL.
Job 1:7

But we are soldiers of God; Christ is our Captain,
We are under His spiritual command.
Engaged in warfare with our adversary the devil,
fighting for the soul of man.

We can't defeat Satan with our intellect
no matter how clever our reasoning.
We can't defeat Satan with our hatred of him,
God's love is the only seasoning.
Matthew 5:44   Romans 13:10
I John 4:7-8

Christ expects us to enter Satan's domain
only after the strong man has been bound.
We can't bind him without the Holy Spirit;
God's love and His doctrine so sound.
Matthew 12:29   John 16:7-13

The devil's devices are many and varied;
they're not new to the person he seeks.
He preys on the area where we are most vulnerable;
he attacks where we are most weak.

He uses *deception, blindness* and *division
unforgiveness, confusion* and *fear,
hatred, disobedience, anxiety* and *worry,*
and the *people* we hold most dear.

For we wrestle not against flesh and blood,
but spiritual wickedness in high places.
Be strong in the Lord, put on the whole armor;
with God we hold all the aces.
Ephesians 6:10-13

We may be troubled on every side,
perplexed, persecuted and cast down.
We are not distressed, in despair or forsaken,
not destroyed because our Lord is around.
II Corinthians 4:8-9

When you feel rejected, hard pressed or grief stricken,
don't lose or abandon your hope.
The Lord will never leave nor forsake;
you are never at the end of your rope.

Measure yourself with Christ as the standard;
it's God's battle and He has your back.
Be a faithful warrior according to God's plan;
about His Word He is not slack.

My problem is patience and material things,
and I'm standing right at the gate.
The word says stand still and see His salvation,
but it seems so hard to just wait.
Exodus 13:14

The word says ask and ye shall receive,
but it's deeper than just getting what you ask.
"My grace is sufficient" means just what it says;
God will take what you have and make it last.
II Corinthians 12:9

I have read the scriptures and, yes, I know
I am to walk by faith not by sight.
I will then experience the fullness of His love,
and know it's not me nor my might.
II Corinthians 5:7

Slowly but surely I'm getting a little better,
I'm learning to perish the thought;
the more I realize that this *free* salvation,
at a very high price, was bought.
Romans Chapters 5 and 8

The same device Satan tried on Christ
is the one that worked on Eve.
Resist the devil and he will flee,
putting his whole operation on freeze.
James 4:7

He will try the same little tricks on us,
so be aware of your weakness and vices.
Lest Satan should get an advantage of us,
be not ignorant of his devices.
II Corinthians 13:5
II Corinthians 2:11

IT'S JUST A MATTER OF TIME

We are children of God and joint heirs with Christ,
yet we've lived a life of sin.
We do not know the day or hour,
so it's time to come on in.
Matthew 24:36

The time is now to serve the Lord,
our past we can't relive.
We can repent with a sincere heart
and God will surely forgive.

There is a time for everything,
every purpose under the sun.
Every knee shall bow in time;
God would have us be as one.
Isaiah 45:23

It's appointed time to man upon earth
and then we all must die.
In the process of time it will come to pass;
until then we all must try.
Job 7:1   Genesis 4:3

To live an obedient and upright life
as examples to sin-sick brothers,
Showing the message of love and Christ,
pointing the way for others.

Whatsoever thy hands findeth to do,
do it with might and be brave.
There is no work, knowledge or wisdom
once you are laid in the grave.
Ecclesiastes 9:10

The race is not given to the swift
nor the battle to the strong.
Time and chance happen to them all,
those right as well as those wrong.
Ecclesiastes 9:11

The rain falls on the just and unjust;
we are made after God's own kind.
He's begun a good work that He will complete,
and it's just a matter of time.
Matthew 5:45
Philippians 1:6

When a picture is painted its very best,
it is called a masterpiece.
That's how God sees each of us
and He wants us to release:

The love of Christ we have inside
our stubborn minds and heart.
We can loose and bind on earth and in heaven
if we will do our part.
Matthew 16:19
Matthew 18:18

If God's people which are called by His name
would humble themselves and pray,
Turn from wicked ways and seek His face,
He will heal our land someday.
II Chronicles 7:14

I believe it's just a matter of time
until each person sees the light.
The Lord will hide us in His pavilion
if we would just get it right.
Psalm 27:5

CONGRATULATIONS
Kim Woodyard

You have shared in the course of a new creation;
train your child in the way they should go,
for you are blessed and highly favored
as only a mother could know.

Yet into each life a tear must fall
from pain and sorrow, maybe,
but yours should be happy tears of joy
welcoming your new baby.

And as we share this Christmas Luncheon,
reflect just for a while
on the reason that we share at all
is the birth of Christ, God's child.

He brought to us a wealth of love
from heaven to earth below,
just as your child is the pot of love
waiting at the end of your bow.

YOU

On this merry Christmas eve
the birth of Christ we cheer.
We pray God's speed for all of you
and those you hold most dear.

This season brings a special message,
but there is nothing new.
Penned today, twelve twenty-four,
it's simply titled

YOU.

Yes; I am the light of the world
and I was born under the law.
The world without me and the love I bring
would be dark, no God, what a flaw.
John 8:12
Galatians 4:4

But your God made a perfect world
and in you He placed His hope.
He gave you the key to all His kingdom;
you fell prey, you sinned, what a dope.
Matthew 16:19
Romans 3:33

When the fullness of time had come,
God sent me His son
To reconcile you back to Him;
He would have us be as one.
Job 33:1-30
II Corinthians 5:20

I left my throne to bring you hope;
I defied all time and space
That you may have an abundant life
and the knowledge of His Grace.
John 10:10

I came to give you peace on earth
with love and goodwill toward men,
To offer you eternal life
by cleansing you from sin.
Luke 2:14

There are some things that you must do —
the first one is to believe.
According to the word that I am the Christ
and your burdens I can relieve.
Hebrew 11:6

It's also a must that you repent
with godly sorrow for your past days.
Confess with your mouth and be baptized,
acknowledge me in all your ways.
Luke 13:3   Acts 2:38
Romans 10:9-10   I John 1:9

You must live an obedient life
according to the word I teach.
I will lead and always guide you
to the person you next must reach.
John 16:13

For it is through you my gospel is shared
and you must go the last mile.
You're the only church some folk will know;
live the word through your lifestyle.

I have given you much and much is required,
and I will be with you till the end.
We depend on each other in this Christian struggle;
for this I call you my friend
Luke 12:48
Matthew 28:20
John 15:13-15

You too can be God's dawn of deliverance,
a ray of light to men.
When their test and trials seem darkest,
it's up to you to step in.

Let them know they are somebody
and show them that you care.
Tell them their faith will make them well
and God will always be there.
Mark 5:34

Whatever their sorrow, whatever their bondage,
whatever their burden or plight,
Let them know when Jesus comes in
He brings gladness, freedom and light.

No matter what the situation is,
when we give our life to Christ,
We can do all things through faith in Him
and never think about it twice.

S.O.S.

A message of warning is not eagerly received
by those who don't have Christ within.
Life is a process of overcoming; and
struggle on this **SEA OF SIN.**

But Christ is in us the hope of glory;
it's up to us to be courageous and bold.
Just like our example; the Lord Jesus Christ;
when He died just to **SAVE OUR SOULS.**

Are you willing to risk who you are as a person
and change your whole life's cultivation?
If you're looking for hope, you can find it in Christ
by living the **SIGNS OF SALVATION.**

Signs of salvation are not just for show;
commitment comes with a cost, count it up.
We're either **SAINT OR SINNER,** not in-between;
we choose with which master we sup.

We either **SERVE OUR SAVIOR**
or **SERVE OLD SATAN;**
they both offer eternal life.
One offers all the promises of God,
the other just misery and strife.

Which are you, a **SERVANT OR SPECTATOR?**
Remember, faith without works is dead.
Your faithfulness will always be rewarded,
but obedience will get you ahead.

DISCIPLING

The ultimate model is Jesus Christ;
to us the Father He shows.
"Come, Follow me," Jesus said,
fish for men from the deepest of throes.
Matthew 4:19-20

When He got in His boat, His disciples followed
and suddenly a great tempest arose.
Waves covered the boat, but Christ was asleep.
"Lord, save us" was the cry from those.
Matthew 8:23-25

Why are you fearful, you of little faith?
He arose and rebuked the storm.
The winds and the sea obeyed His voice
and immediately there was a great calm.
Matthew 8:26-27

He explained and coached as He led the way;
they experimented and applied what was taught.
They received their commission to go and represent,
for our lives, with His life, was being bought.

He was more than a teacher of skill and attitude,
He imparted a Holy lifestyle.
Everything God gave Him, He gave to those
that would follow Him the very last mile.

We will have to endure until the end
in order that we be saved.
Christ is our example, stay focused on Him
because the road to Glory, He paved.

A disciple is not above his teacher,
but every student who is perfectly trained
will imitate his teacher in all that he does
and in his fellowship will remain.
Luke 6:40

THE LIGHT

Jesus came down from Heaven above
bearing the torch of truth.
Without the love and light He brings,
our lives would be of no use.

Without the light of Jesus
in the world that we live in,
We would have eternal darkness,
doomed forever to a life of sin.

But because He is the light of the world,
the Promised Savior from above,
Those who follow shall not walk in darkness
but in the light of His love.
John 8:12

Let your light so shine among men
like Christ's light glowed for you,
So that men may see your many good works
in the numerous things that you do.
Matthew 5:16

Your works should glorify your Father in Heaven
for it's Him that life is all about.
Having faith, yes, but not in yourself,
believing in Him with no doubt.

Sin is never worth the trouble
that it bring in a person's life.
If your riches increase, take a look at your heart
and remember that you are the wife.
Psalm 62:10

Christ is the head, you are to follow His lead;
keep in mind that He is the light.
He is the strength of your life, be of good courage,
wait on Him to set it right.
Psalm 27:1 and 14

HE

He was in the world that was made by him,
but the world he made didn't know
from whence he came, or who he was,
or the places he would go.
John 1:10

Yet he started his journey young and alone,
in Jerusalem during customs of the feast.
He tarried behind and his parents knew not,
but he was schooling the doctors and the priest.
Luke 2:42-46

He came unto his own and they received him not;
throughout history that's the way it has been.
The objective was not to condemn, but instead,
to save man from his own sin.
John 1:11
John 3:17

He was light unto this darkened world,
a beam of hope for us.
All that he asks is our faith in him,
our obedience and our trust.

If we really knew who Jesus was
and what we have through him,
our view of things would most certainly change,
our glass darkly wouldn't be so dim.
I Corinthians 13:12
Philippians 4:13   John 10:30

If we could comprehend the love of Christ
from his birth, through death, to resurrection,
We could shape tomorrow's world
by what we teach today,
by using his word for correction.
Ephesians 3:17-19
Proverbs 4:10-11

THIS STRANGE PLACE

Birth   =   The Awakening Place
Life   =   The Learning Place
Death   =   The Resting Place
Resurrection   =   The Eternal Place

When all we ever need is in our face,
it never seems to be enough.
We reflect but a moment, then we build
larger barns to hold all of our stuff.
Luke 12:16-21

Seek ye first the kingdom of God,
for therein is his righteousness.
We do things backward and place God last,
we miss out, when we could have been blessed.
Matthew 6:33

I am come in my father's name,
and ye receive me not.
I offer to you eternal life,
but you look for some kind of a plot.
John 5:43

I say follow me, I'll make you fishers of men,
but that's not what you choose to do.
You enjoy my blessings without spreading my gospel,
you act like it's all about you.
Matthew 4:19

I ask you to pray, pray without ceasing,
and to turn from your wicked ways.
You do just the opposite, you cease to pray,
yet you wonder why I shorten some days.
I Thessalonians 5:17   II Chronicles 7:14

I am come that you might have life
and have life more abundantly.
The thief come to steal, kill and destroy,
but it's like him that you want to be.
John 10:10

I am the resurrection and the life,
I have showered you with mercy and grace.
I left you my word and the Holy Spirit,
to lead and guide you through this strange place.
John 11:25-25

Our birth is the place where our eyes are opened,
where we really first become awake
To the things of God through the works of Christ,
and desire of His love to partake.

You were trained as a child in the way you should go,
your whole life is just a place to learn.
To glorify God, praise and lift Him up,
for the meat of His word you should yearn.
Proverbs 22:6   Ephesians 5:20
Hebrews 13:15

Every person you meet wants to go to heaven;
yet no one wants to die.
To live is Christ, to die is gain,
if we only give His way a try.
Philippians 1:21-24

Death is merely a place of rest;
I have asked you to die unto self.
That simply means putting your wants last,
and getting Father's business off the shelf.

I have prepared a place eternal in heaven,
if you can pass the last inspection.
You must endure until the end;
eternal life begins at resurrection.

THEY CARED ENOUGH TO SHARE

For unto us a child is born,
and the world won't be the same.
Wonderful, Counselor, The Mighty God,
The Prince of Peace his name.
Isaiah 9:6

Unto us a son is given,
the government is upon his shoulder.
He's God's only son, come to save the world,
no man will ever be bolder.

For God so loved the world he had made,
He gave his only begotten son,
Not to condemn, but to fulfill,
because the Father and Son are one.
John 3:16   John 10:30
Romans 10:4   Matthew 5:17

They cared enough to give of themselves,
the world was unaware.
Father gave Son and the Son gave his life;
they cared enough to share.
John 3:16   Romans 5:8   I Peter 2:24

Now what has that to do with you?
A question that some may ask.
Well, it's for you that the price was paid,
why He took on such a task.
Mark 10:45

He did it because He loved you,
and the choice was His to make.
Now you have a choice to accept that gift,
and of His love partake.

The Holy Spirit was left with us,
to comfort and abide within,
to reveal all truth, to lead and guide
and to steer us clear of sin.
John 14:26

The question is, do you care enough?
Do you have ears to hear?
Is Jesus Christ your Savior and Lord?
Do you reverence Him with fear?
Ecclesiastes 12:13

Do you care enough to share?
To give of yourself to others?
It's more than the tenth of that which you earn,
it's your heart, and your love for your brothers.

Suppose Christ only gave a tenth,
where would that leave you and I?
We are to follow the example He set,
and yes, that means we must die.
Hebrew 9:27

Now whether we live or whether we die,
our choice, to us, He give.
We are commanded to die unto self
to look to Him and live.
John 6:33

I believe God wants a share of our time,
our talents, our abilities, our skills.
Not just a tenth of what we earn;
going by the old law only kills.
Acts 13:38-39
Romans 10:4
Isaiah 53:11-12

Christ ushered in a new dispensation,
and He paid the ultimate price.
He cared enough to give all He had,
and that included the tithe.

He was reared a rural builder's son.
Yes, He was born in a manger.
From the time the star first appeared in the East,
His life was in constant danger.
Matthew 13:55
Mark 6:3

Silver and gold He had none,
no clout, no wealth, no rank,
but He set himself to the noblest of goals,
disclosing God point-blank.

He seemed strange, distinctive, special, new,
who He really was, was unclear.
But He healed, consoled and lifted up,
prescribing "Peace, Good Cheer."
Matthew 14:27
John 16:33

He proclaimed "Good News" among the poor,
the oppressed, the weak, the lame.
He released the captives from bonds of despair;
we are why He came.
Luke 4:18

He cared enough to surrender His will,
and He only asks us to love,
while He intercedes with God our Father,
where they wait for us above.
Mark 12:31

Christians are like farmers sowing seed,
but our fields are the hearts of man.
We're working for the Kingdom of Heaven,
just doing the best we can.
Matthew 13:24

We are former sinners now born again,
our direction is now toward Christ.
We are still not free from faults or temptations,
but don't commit the same mistake twice.

It doesn't matter how late you started this journey
or how far you feel behind.
If you have repented, you are on your way;
your life style and the word must align.

We are called to be faithful, obey God;
all He wants is our best.
Failure is not final for a born-again believer;
keep the faith, it's only a test.

You must care enough to endure till the end;
there the same shall be saved.
Don't try to fool God, He knows your thoughts and intents;
the road has already been paved.
Matthew 24:13
Mark 13:13

Whatever problems you have, cast them on Christ,
for He certainly cares for you,
but you can't live just any kind of way,
there are some things that you have to do.
I Peter 5:7

Check the Plan of Salvation that's found in the word;
If you care, that's the place to start.
Acknowledge, repent, confess, believe, be baptized,
live a life of love from the heart.

Like the Father, Son and Holy Spirit,
who cared enough to share,
because life consists not in abundance of things,
but serving the Lord in prayer.
Luke 12:15
Romans 12:9-13

So I say through the grace that's given to me,
God bless you, each and every one.
Care enough to share, but give God the Glory
during your faithful walk with the Son.

The Disciple's Mission

Intro

> A disciple's mission is to glorify God
> and to do like Jesus did.
> To be a Kingdom Masterbuilder,
> our gifts can't just lay hid.

Week I

> If we are seeking to master life,
> we must right the wrong we've done.
> Be obedient to Christ, that's our first move,
> in deciding to follow the son.

Week II

> We witness and disciple through relationships,
> not just the sermons we give.
> If we're really saved, we're commanded to witness,
> and it's through the lives we live.

Week III

> Like newborn babies, crave pure spiritual milk,
> we must nurture a new believer.
> Obey what Christ taught, encourage and follow up,
> and be mindful, there is a deceiver.
> *I Peter 2:2-3*

Week IV

> A maturing disciple lives a lifestyle of love,
> for this is the Bible's whole story.
> That we be in Christ, and that Christ be in us,
> which is the Hope Of Glory.
> *Colossians 1:27*

Week V
> As we train other disciples, we depend on Christ;
> He's the model and He passed the test.
> If we act in self we will gain not one,
> even when we give it our best.

Week VI
> He has given us gifts to complete our task;
> we were born with talents and skills.
> Christ ushered in a new dispensation,
> going by the old law only kills.
> *Romans 12:6-10*
> *II Corinthians 3:6*

> Spiritual gifts are not special rewards,
> reserved for the spiritual elite.
> Every believer is given gifts,
> when they lay it all (life) at His feet.
> *I Corinthians 12:1-31*

Summary
> Each disciple has a cross to bear,
> and they certainly won't weigh the same.
> The bottom line is to give God the Glory;
> don't look to yourself for fame.
> *Proverbs 3:6*
> *Ecclesiastes 9:11*

> Seek ye first the kingdom of God;
> spend quality time with the Master.
> There's a biblical process for growing disciples,
> any other way is disaster.
> *Matthew 6:33*

There will be some victories and some defeats;
all God wants is our best.
Failure is not final for a born-again believer,
keep the faith, it's only a test.

Live in the word, pray in faith,
fellowship and minister to others.
The life we live is a witness to the world,
don't be an offense to our brothers.

B.E.L.I.E.V.E.
Behind Enemy Lines in Earthen Vessels Expecting

Ye shall hear of wars and rumors of wars;
these things must come to pass.
The end is not yet if you are in Christ,
if you watch and in faith you stand fast.
Matthew 24:6, 13
I Corinthians 16:13

Endure the hardness as a good soldier;
each person must count up the cost.
The fields of battle are our hearts and minds,
and the Captain wants no man to be lost.
II Timothy 2:3   Luke 15:28, 31
II Peter 3:9

There is a time of war and a time of peace,
and it is first conceived in our minds.
Prepare yourself, put on your armor,
you're going behind enemy lines.
Ecclesiastes 3:8   Ephesians 6:11-18

You will wrestle not against flesh and blood,
but wickedness in high places.
Let this mind be in you, which was also in Christ,
no matter what the situation or cases.
Ephesians 6:12   Philippians 2:5

He that cometh to God must believe that He is,
that he'll reward them that diligently seek.
When behind enemy lines it's best to be quiet,
be firm, but humble and meek.
Hebrew 5:5   I Timothy 6:13
Matthew 27:11-14   Matthew 5:5
Psalm 149:4

Joseph the dreamer was Israel's son,
with a coat of many colors.
He was loved more than the other children
and was hated by the rest of his brothers.
Genesis 37:3-5

He told them of a dream that he had dreamed,
and they hated him all the more.
Jealousy and envy overtook them;
to sin they had opened the door.
Genesis 37:5-11

Joseph the dreamer went looking for his brothers,
who were out with the flocks to feed.
A certain man found him wandering in the field,
and asked him, "What Is Thy Need?"
Genesis 37:15

I seek for my brothers, where they feed their flock,
my father wants to know if they're fine.
They conspired to slay him on the fields of Dothan;
he was now behind the enemy's line.
Genesis 37:14-18

Joseph was sold by his brothers to merchants,
sold again to the captain of the guard.
A lie was concocted and told unto Israel,
who took the bad news very hard.
Genesis 37:28-36

The Lord was with Joseph and he was prosperous
in all that he put his hand.
He was a goodly person who was well favored,
but Joseph was still just a man.
Genesis 39:2-6

The master's wife cast her eyes on Joseph.
She said, "Lie With Me," day by day.
He refused her offer and fled from her presence;
He went safely, he thought, on his way.
Genesis 39:7-12

In his haste to leave Joseph left his garment,
and the woman formed a plan in her mind.
She lied to her husband about Joseph's intentions;
he was deeper behind enemy lines.
Genesis 39:12-20

Again the Lord was with Joseph and showed him mercy;
all the prisoners were committed to his lot.
He interpreted dreams for two of the men;
upon release the chief butler forgot.
Genesis 39:21— Genesis 40:23

And it came to pass at the end of two years,
Pharaoh dreamed and didn't know what it meant.
The chief butler remembered his time in prison,
and for Joseph, the King of Egypt sent.
Genesis 41:1-14

Pharaoh's dreams were interpreted by Joseph,
as seven good years and seven bad.
Pharaoh took off his ring and placed it on Joseph,
making him ruler over all that Egypt had.
Genesis 41:15-44

Now Moses kept the flock of his in-law father,
and the angel of the Lord appeared.
A bush burned aflame but was not consumed,
not even one leaf was seared.
Exodus 3:1-3

God called unto Moses from the midst of the bush
and said you're standing on holy ground.
I am come to deliver my children of Israel
from Egypt where they are currently bound.
Exodus 3:4-9

Come now, therefore, and I will send you,
that thou mayest get my people free.
Moses said to God, "Who Am I To Go?"
Who shall I say sent me?
Exodus 3:10-13

Say I am that I am has sent me to you;
go and bring all the elders to meet.
I will bring you out of the misery of Egypt;
milk and honey will flow at your feet.
Exodus 3:14-17

I am sure the king of Egypt will not let you go,
and I will smite them with all my wonders.
It shall come to pass that he will let you go,
and all his deeds will be as blunders.
Exodus 3:19-21

Moses was being sent behind enemy lines,
and he kept trying to find an excuse.
He finally had to go with his brother Aaron,
because complaining to God was no use.
Exodus 4:1-31

On enemy territory, behind enemy lines,
many plagues were brought on the land.
The Lord had hardened Pharaoh's heart,
and many wonders were done at Moses' hand.
Exodus 5:1— Exodus 11:10

Finally the captives fled from Egypt;
Pharaoh's army all drowned in the sea.
Three days later the people murmured and complained,
and the Lord showed Moses a tree.
Exodus 12:30 — Exodus 15:25

Bitter water made sweet and bread from heaven,
but the people wanted flesh to eat.
And so it was, but because of disobedience,
there was a price to be paid for the meat.
Exodus 15:25 — Exodus 16:22
Numbers 11:7-35

Women were sent to entice Sampson,
to learn a riddle and the source of his might.
Sampson had a weakness for the opposite sex,
and this is what caused his plight.
Judges 13-16

He was a Nazarite to God from the womb,
no razor was to come on his head.
His task was to begin to deliver Israel,
but he seemed to go from bed to bed.

Was Sampson lured behind his enemies' line?
Or was this a secret part of God's plan?
The Philistines were defeated by the mighty Sampson,
and many thousands died at his hand.

Sampson called on God, "Lord, Remember Me,"
strengthen me this once, I pray,
That I may be avenged of the Philistines,
and let me die with them today.

Daniel was found praying to his Lord and God,
the window open to his chambers, on his knee.
A conspiracy was formed to have Daniel killed,
because praying was against the decree.
Daniel Chapter 6

Daniel was cast into the lions' den;
the King's signet sealed the stone.
The Lord sent his angels because Daniel believed,
and he suffered not one broken bone.

King Nebuchadnezzar made an idol god,
an image that was made of gold.
He decreed that every person would bow and worship,
or he would burn them in the furnace like coal.
Daniel Chapter 3

The Hebrew boys believed that the God they served
would deliver them free from the fire.
If it be so, or if it be not,
whichever was the Lord's desire.

The three Jewish men refused to bow down,
and the king had to settle the score.
All three were cast into the fiery furnace,
but lo and behold were seen four.

Who was that fourth man, walking loose,
with no hurt, to him or the three?
The fourth had a form like the Son of God,
and the king had to change his decree.

Jesus was also behind enemy lines,
but He did not have to be.
He volunteered for this temporary duty,
on a mission to set us free.

He was led of the Spirit into the wilderness,
where He fasted forty days and nights.
There He was tempted by the devil,
but He held to His faith, not his sight.
Matthew 4:1-11

In the book of Matthew, chapter twenty six,
where the rulers made plans to kill,
They did not believe that Jesus was the Christ,
and He was ready for Calvary's hill.
Matthew 26:

Christ was betrayed and He was denied,
and many false witnesses came.
Jesus held His peace but He was accused;
yet in Him there was no blame.
Matthew 26:

Jesus was bound and taken to the governor,
but Pilate just washed his hands.
He said, "Behold, I bring Him forth unto you,
I find no fault in the man."
Matthew 27:1-24
John 19:1-4

Jesus was deep behind enemy lines,
but this was all part of God's plan,
To reconcile mankind back to God,
and it had to be through one man.

Because through one man was paradise lost,
one man had to make amends.
Jesus was the scapegoat for all the world,
and shed His blood for remission of sin.
Matthew 26:28

Christ was crucified, died, and was buried,
but He rose with all power in His hand.
He knew and believed in God His Father
and kept focused on His mission and plan.

As new babes in Christ or seasoned believers,
we all go behind the enemy's line.
It's part of the training for being a good soldier,
being committed, body, soul and mind.

All people mentioned in this poem
have at least a few things the same.
They were all earthen vessels chosen by God,
to operate things in His name.

Each one believed, each one expected
that God would do all He said.
Each was a living testimony for us,
to **BELIEVE** and let God be the head.

DIVINE INTERVENTION

Jesus sat wearied at Jacob's well,
and it was noon, about the sixth hour.
There cometh a woman to draw some water,
but got a sample of Jesus' power.
John 4:6-7

Wearied from His journey as he sat on the well,
Jesus saith to her, "Give me to drink."
She was a woman of Samaria, Jesus a Jew,
what would all the people think?
John 4:6-9

Jesus answered, "If you knew the gift of God,
and who it is you're talking to,
you would ask of him for living water,"
and accomplish what he asks you to do.
John 4:10

She asked for the water that she thirst not,
and Jesus began to give her the word.
He told her who he was, about the Spirit and the Truth;
She went and told everything that she heard.
John 4:15-29

Because she believed and then testified,
many more believed because of His word.
Not from her saying, that He was The Christ,
but indeed it was The Christ they heard.
John 4:39-42

Preachers can preach and choirs can sing,
but you must seek the Lord for yourself.
It's you that is lost, not Jesus The Christ;
He calls you but you act like you're deaf.

As far as the woman coming to the well,
being saved was not her intention.
But Jesus of necessity went through Samaria,
an example of Divine intervention.
John 4:4

She had five husbands and was then shacking up,
when she met at the well the Teacher.
She perceived He was a prophet, then she believed,
and she went from prostitute to preacher.
John 4:18-19

In Mary Magdalene there were seven devils
that were cast out, I don't know by whom.
But Mary believed in Jesus The Christ
and was first to see Him, waiting at the tomb.
Luke 8:2   John 20:1-2 and 11-18

With seven devils in her, surely she sinned,
at least while the devils were present.
But after knowing Jesus and believing on Him,
Mary went from sinner to servant.

Saul was making havoc of the church,
committing all the Christians to jail.
Though he did it through ignorance and unbelief,
he was humbled on the Damascus trail.
Acts 8:3 I Timothy 1:13 Acts 9:3-6

He, trembling and astonished, said to the Lord,
"What wilt Thou have me to do?"
The Lord said, "Arise, and go to the city,
and there it will be told of you."
Acts 9:6

God chose him as a vessel to bear His name,
to send him throughout all the land.
He showed him many great things he must suffer;
Saul became a Christian man.
Acts 9:15:16

The majority of the books in the New Testament
were written by a man named Paul.
One and the same, Saul of Tarsus,
after he answered the Lord and Master's call.
Acts 9:11   Acts 13:9   Acts 9:6

From sinner to saint is where Paul went.
Who would have thought he could change so much?
It was divine intervention on the road to Damascus,
when the Holy Spirit reached out to touch.
Acts 9:4-5

Moses grew up in Egypt,
even though he was Hebrew.
He saw an Egyptian punishing his brethren,
and into a rage he flew.
Exodus 2:11

Moses killed the Egyptian,
and he hid him in the sand.
Pharaoh heard and sought to kill Moses,
but Moses had fled from the land.
Exodus 2:12-15

An angel appeared unto Moses
in a bush aflame with fire.
He was ordered back into Egypt,
for his brothers' situation was dire.
Exodus 3:1-10

I know you have heard the story
about Pharaoh and the parting sea.
Moses went from murderer to missionary,
as he helped to set the captives free.
Exodus 3-20

A man named Job was perfect and upright;
he was greatest of all men of the east.
But there was a test brother Job had to take,
where he would go from most to the least.
Job 1:1-3, 8

Have thou considered my servant Job?
A perfect and an upright man.
All that he has is in your power,
but upon him put forth not your hand.
Job 1:8-12

Job lost all that a man could lose,
his property, his family, his friends,
But he held fast to his faith in God,
and he was blessed in the latter end.
Job 19:25-26
Job 42:10-17

From chieftain to charity, from most to least,
from riches to rags is the story.
By divine intervention our God comes through,
and we go on from glory to glory.

MASK THE MISERY

When you're walking along and you meet someone,
you greet them and they say, "I'm fine."
Have you ever wondered if they're telling the truth,
or masking their misery by lying?

Maybe even you have done it yourself,
answered questions by pure reflex.
You didn't mean to lie, it was force of habit,
and may even be out of context.

Is there always, but always, a smile on your face,
no matter how bad you might feel?
Masking the misery can also be a habit,
if you would let Jesus be real.

Since you are a vessel that's been washed clean
in His blood through his mercy and grace,
Let Him fill you with love, till you overflow,
that love will take your misery's place.
Psalm 51:2   II Timothy 2:9-21
Romans 9:21-23

Christ will clean you up, if you desire to be clean,
He will fill you with His love if you ask,
But you must first come to yourself;
do you want to be first or last?
Matthew 7:7   Mark 10:31
Luke 15:17

He asks that you cast your cares upon Him,
and your burdens He will share.
If you come unto him with a sincere heart,
and at the altar leave your problems there.
I Peter 5:7   Psalm 55:22

Satan wants your heart because it holds God's law,
so he steadily plays tricks with your mind
To keep you off track and entangled with the world,
at the rapture you'll be left behind.
Jeremiah
I John 2:15-17

Out of the heart are the issues of life,
with all diligence the heart we must keep.
Though fragmented and frail, we can mask the misery
by laying it at the Savior's feet.
Proverbs 4:23

Some people appear calm and serene on the surface,
like a duck as it gracefully goes,
But under the surface there's a lot of turbulence,
as it paddles those little webbed toes.

Are you paddling on the pond of life,
striving for that distant shore?
Mask your misery in the love of God,
with Christ the Savior as core.
Romans 13:10

He is the foundation, the chief cornerstone,
the one many people reject.
Without him we can do nothing;
Christ Jesus is God's elect.
Psalm 118:22   Ephesians 2:20
Romans 8:28-33   John 17:22
John 15:5

SHOW ME THE WAY

1. *Proverbs 16:7*   When a man's ways please the Lord, he maketh even his enemies to be at peace with him.

2. *Jeremiah 6:16*   Thus saith the Lord, Stand ye in the ways, and see, and ask for the old paths, where is the good way, and walk therein, and ye shall find rest for your souls. But they said, we will not walk therein.

3. *Jeremiah 10:2-3*   Thus saith the Lord, learn not the way of the heathen, (3) for the customs of the people are vain.

4. *Isaiah 55:6-9*   Seek ye the Lord while he may be found, call upon him while he is near: (7) let the wicked forsake his ways, and the righteous man his thoughts: and let him return unto the Lord, and he will have mercy upon him; and to our God, for he will abundantly pardon. (8) For my thoughts are not your thoughts, neither are your ways my ways, saith the Lord. (9) For as the heavens are higher than the earth, so are my ways higher than your ways, and my thoughts than your thoughts.

5. *Proverbs 16:25*   There is a way that seemeth right unto a man; but the end thereof are the ways of death.

6. *Deut. 5:33*   Ye shall walk in all the ways which the Lord your God hath commanded you, that ye may live, and that it may be well with you, and that ye may prolong your days in the land which ye shall possess.

7. *Deut. 8:6*   Therefore thou shalt keep the commandments of the Lord thy God, to walk in his ways, and to fear him.

8. *Deut. 10:12*   And now, Israel, what doth the Lord thy God require of thee, but to fear the Lord thy God, to walk in all his ways, and to love him, and to serve the Lord thy God with all thy heart and with all thy soul.

9. *Deut. 11:22*   For if ye shall diligently keep all these commandments which I command you, to do them, to love the Lord your God, to walk in all his ways, and to cleave unto him.

10. *Jeremiah 16:17*   For mine eyes are upon all their ways: they are not hid from my face, neither is their inequity hid from my eyes.

11. *Jeremiah 17:10*   I the Lord search the heart, I try the reins, even to give every man according to his ways, and according to the fruits of his doings.

12. *Isaiah 30:21*   And thine ears shall hear a word
                      behind thee, saying, this is the way,
                      walk ye in it, when ye turn to the
                      right hand, and when ye turn to the
                      left.

13. Haggai 1:5-7   Now therefore thus saith the Lord
                      of hosts; consider your ways. (6) Ye
                      have sown much, and bring in
                      little, ye eat, but ye have not
                      enough; ye drink, but ye are not
                      filled with drink; ye clothe you, but
                      there is not warm; and he that
                      earneth wages to put into a bag
                      with holes. (7) Thus saith the Lord
                      of hosts; consider your ways.

14. *Psalm 39:1*   I said, I will take heed to my ways,
                      that I sin not with my tongue: I will
                      keep my mouth with a bridle, while
                      the wicked is before me.

15. *Jeremiah 7:3*   Thus saith the Lord of host, the
                      God of Israel, amend your ways
                      and your doings, and I will cause
                      you to dwell in this place.

16. *Psalm 32:8*   I will instruct thee and teach thee
                      in the way which thou shalt go: I
                      will guide thee with mine eye.

SHOW ME THE WAY

Father God, as I study your word
at the close of a long hard day,
I pray for forgiveness for all my sins;
continue to show me the way.

I was wandering as a blind man in the streets;
I had ears but I did not hear.
I knew of the awesome power of God,
but in my heart there was no fear.

Your ways were not mine, neither your thoughts.
I was out of control, at best,
But through your word, which now shows me the way,
my experiences in the world were a test.

I have returned unto you, thank you for mercy,
for your grace and your abundant pardon.
Thank you for being so patient with me,
and not allowing my heart to harden.

Lord God, I know what's required of me
is to fear you and walk in your ways,
To love and to serve with all my heart and soul;
it's the process that prolongs my days.

I pray, Lord God, that you show me the way;
help me examine and amend what I do.
Renew a right spirit, help me grow in your love,
that my ways will be pleasing to you.

I call on you, Lord, while you are near;
please hear me, I long to be found.
I forsake my thoughts and wicked ways,
and I want to be heaven bound.

Turn my heart from the heathen way,
for the customs of the people are vain.
The way that seemeth right unto me, a man,
are the ways of death and sheer pain.

Instruct me, teach me, help me bridle my tongue,
inside me I want you to dwell.
Create in me a clean heart O God,
so that all with me may be well.

I have the desire to please you Lord.
And find rest for my weary soul.
I'll stand in your ways and walk therein,
they are good, Father help me be bold.

I want to serve you Lord and cleave unto you,
and love with all my mind, soul, and heart.
I pray your help in amending my doings,
show me the way, where to start.

For others like me, Father I intercede,
that they come to themselves some day.
And return unto Father, like the Prodigal Son,
I pray you will show us the way.

ABIDE (LIVE) IN THE WORD

To develop a close relationship,
you must live in the Word.
Being a disciple is a faith process
that cannot be shirked or deferred.

For all your decisions, seek his guidance
as you petition for needs each day.
This is disciple training at work
where you must abide and obey.
Proverbs 3:5-6

Abide in him and he in you;
you are a branch, he's the vine.
You cannot produce except you're connected,
and it's vanity for you to keep trying.
John 15:4-7

You see he is the Way, the Truth and the Life;
He was in the beginning with God.
It's in him you live, move and have being,
and really his way is not hard.
John 14:6   John 1:1   Acts 17:28

He has set before you life and death;
you have the option of choice.
Hold to his teaching and he'll set you free,
but you must obey only his voice.
John 8:31-32   Deuteronomy 30:10-16

He speaks to you in many ways'
Those who have ears should hear.
If you are his sheep you will know his voice
and will come unto him without fear.
John 10:1-5   Revelations 2:7

Pastors, preachers, evangelists, teachers,
they all tell you what he say,
But the most effective message delivered
is revealed through your study each day.
Ephesians 4:11-12
II Timothy 2:15

The Holy Word is your life abide in it,
be committed and remain in his love.
Obey his commands as he did his Father,
and you too will soon rise above.
John 15:10

Discipling is not a one-time event;
being a Christian is a life-long deal.
It's a process of trials, failures and overcoming,
where you learn that God's love is for real.

It will cause you to examine yourself,
were you are and where you want to go.
Abide in the word, walk daily with the Son;
He's your guide, your passage, He'll know.
II Corinthians 13:5

THIS IS YOUR LIFE

When Jesus came in the form of a man.
He already knew the price,
For He was in the beginning with God
and knew He was the coming Christ.
John 1:1-3   John 6:38
Hebrew 10:5

He is the way, the truth, and the life;
He is the word made flesh.
All things that were made, were made by him
and mankind was his best.
John 14:6   John 1:14
Genesis 1:1

He made man in his image and
placed man in charge of all.
He knew then that the flesh was weak,
and man would eventually fall.
Genesis 1:26
Matthew 26:41

So in the great grand scheme of things
let there never be any doubt,
While he was making all that was made,
he also made us a way out.
Genesis 2:9
Genesis 3:24

He knew the thief would someday come
to steal, to kill, to destroy;
He prepared himself to give his own life
so that you and I would have joy.
John 10:10
John 10:17-18

He came that we have abundant life
in the flesh and the spirit as well.
Life is more than raiment and meat;
it is dying, yet living, without hell.
John 10:10
Luke 12:22-23

To die is gain when you really find life
and you are crucified with him.
Obtain his favor, abide in his word,
and worry not about any of them.
Proverbs 8:35
Philippians 2:21

He came from heaven as the bread of life
and said eat, for this is my body.
This reference is to the Holy Word
that we often take so melancholy.
John 6:48-54
Matthew 26:26

Except we eat we have no life;
we must get this word within
or else we starve our spirit man
and our flesh man leads us to sin.
John 6:56
Romans 6:12-18

He is our light and our salvation;
his word is his will and his way.
He's the living bread, our life's sustainer;
all we need do is obey.
Psalms 27:1
John 6:57-58

Is it hard to believe that his word is our life?
The truth that's so simple and plain.
Even a fool can understand, if he want,
that with Christ, everything we can gain.
Matthew 4:4

This is our life, His Holy Word,
and we seem to take it for granted.
Let every man examine himself
and see what in his heart has been planted.
Psalms 119:25
II Corinthians 13

We know for sure the incorruptible seed
can lie dormant in a deceitful heart
Until it is hallowed by the Holy Spirit
and each person has done his / her part.
I Corinthians 15:53-58

Your part is to choose, choose life today
because you know not what is for tomorrow.
What is your life, it is even a **vapor,**
a little time that He let you borrow.
Deuteronomy 30:19
James 4:13-15

Your life is not yours, it is hid with Christ;
when you borrow you're supposed to pay back.
He gave us life, He just loaned us the time,
how did we ever get so far off track?
Colossians 3:1-4

SPIRITUALLY BANKRUPT
Rich in Death, Destitute in Life

We lived our lives the way we chose;
bad choices were the order of the day.
We took no thought of our Lord Jesus Christ,
him being the truth, the life and the way.
John 14:6

In the middle of our lives we are blessed with plenty,
we eat, we drink, we are merry.
With our barns full of goods, we take our ease,
we say to our souls, "Don't worry."
Luke 12:16-19

Yesterday is gone, tomorrow is not promised;
the only time we have is today,
to cease from our wisdom, labor not to be rich,
and begin doing things God's way.
Proverbs 23:4

If we lay up treasures just for ourselves,
and we don't become rich toward Christ,
when our soul is required, at some unknown time,
we go away full of sorrow, what a price.
Luke 12:20-21

The love of money is the root of all evil;
where your treasure is, so is your heart.
For they that be rich, a snare is set,
and they drown in destruction for their part.
I Timothy 6:9-10
Matthew 6:21

Because you say that you are rich,
and your goods are increased beyond measure,
You have need of nothing, but really you're blind;
you are naked and miserable, with no treasure.
Revelation 3:17

Give and it shall be given to you,
good measure pressed down, shaken up.
With the measure ye mete, it shall be measured to you,
and it will over run your cup.
Luke 6:38

God said in His word to give to the poor,
follow him and have heavenly treasure.
If you want to be perfect, give up your possessions,
follow Christ and do His spiritual pleasure.
Matthew 19:21-22

In the secular world you can reorganize,
or you can file for liquidation,
either farm, business, or as an individual,
for your bad under-estimation.

For your lack of knowledge or over-extending,
or maybe it was greed or pride.
Whatever the reason for filing bankruptcy,
life is just not a free ride.
Hosea 4:6

You can get some help from your trustee,
with making a financial plan,
based on your assets, your debts and your needs,
but eventually you have to face the man.

You can file chapter seven or chapter twelve,
or file under eleven or thirteen.
The bottom line will be a lifestyle change,
because you're trying to get your record clean.

It's really similar in the spiritual realm,
except here it's called the rebirth,
and everything is on an individual basis,
and have nothing to do with your worth.

Your reasons for having to face the man
will be the same in either case.
The one exception, in the spiritual realm,
Christ Jesus has taken your place.

Unlike the trustee with a financial plan,
Christ's plan is the one of salvation.
He gave his life on the Cross at Calvary,
when He died for every man, every nation.

The bottom line will also be the same
which is a change in your way of life.
You're still trying to get your record clean
and be relieved of some misery and strife.

If you are bankrupt in your spirit,
just what is left to take?
Christ the Savior, your only true judge,
will intercession for you make.
Romans 8:34

When you come to yourself, after wasting your spoils,
and you have no other place to go,
Remember your Father and His Son Jesus Christ,
they who sit high and look low.
Luke 15:11-24

You are always afforded another chance
to be rid of the debts of your past.
File with Christ Jesus in the 3-4-U option;
it's the plan that will eternally last.

This plan has never, never failed,
but you must endure till the end.
Even though you are free, it's like being on probation,
and you are constantly tempted by sin.
Matthew 24:13

Once you have filed there are certain limitations,
some things you can no longer do.
Like credit applications in the secular world,
here, sin is off limits to you.

Your circle of friends will most likely change
after filing bankruptcy with Christ.
Committing totally to Him, with your flesh subjected,
you will turn from your sin and your vice.

RONALD R. SMITH

A tree is known by the fruit it bears
and comes forth in its season;
there is a time for everything,
the Comforter knows the reason.

Ron was placed in the earth with us;
his presence blessed us like no other.
One thing we all can say about Ron:
he treated everyone like a brother.

He went out of his way to help other people;
it didn't matter if they were young or old;
In every situation where you observed his action,
Ron was a man under control.

Ron would always carefully listen,
then he would make his point with a smile.
He never seemed angry, but you got his message;
he would go with you the last mile.

God places in our path many individuals,
and through them He reveals himself.
Ron never boasted, he lived a life of love;
his love was not sitting on a shelf.

Like Michaelangelo's painting in the Sistine Chapel
of God extending a hand toward man,
that's the way Ron was to all of us;
let's follow his example, and we can.

All of us today have another chance
to be rid of the debts of our past.
The first step is, we must repent
make investments with Christ, they last.

He has a 3-4-U Plan that has never failed,
but you must endure till the end,
You withdraw and deposit through the Holy Spirit
as you turn from your vice and your sin.

Ron will be missed, but this too will pass;
we all have to go this way.
Make the transition easy, give your life to Christ;
you need to make this decision today.

KENNETH L. NATIONS

I know your road seems rough today,
but this is only a test.
You're starting a new chapter in life;
Believe me, the Father knows best.

New doors are being opened, old ones closed;
you'll be making some changes in life.
You're gaining a friend in Jesus the Lord;
you're not really losing a wife.

Although it hurts, this too will pass,
for God will see you through.
Cast your cares upon Him today,
and trust Him in all you do.
Proverbs 3:6
I Peter 5:7

Your problems may seem like the highest mountain,
but they are nothing compared to some.
Consider Moses, Job, and what Jesus went through;
in the end you see who won.

I'm praying that you will trust in God,
lean not to your own understanding.
Seek ye first the kingdom of God,
and follow what He is commanding.
Matthew 6:33
Proverbs 3:5

And no, I didn't forget your leave,
I got your back for the rest of the week,
but Jesus has your back forever;
just look to Him and be meek.

PORTRAIT OF A MAN

Try seeing yourself as God sees you,
not as you are but how you can be.
Though bound with trouble, a life of sin,
God sees you set free.
I Samuel 16:7

He made you in His image from dust,
and gave you the breath of life.
You then became a living soul,
and He provided for you a wife.
Genesis 1:26
Genesis 2:7-9

He planted a garden eastward in Eden,
and in charge He placed the man,
with dominion over all that God had made,
with free will to follow God's plan.

Every tree that is pleasant to the sight,
and every tree for food that is good
was made to grow in this beautiful garden,
and man could live forever if he would.

For the tree of life was in the midst of the garden,
the tree of knowledge of good and bad.
Man was commanded what he *should not* do,
but he was not satisfied with what he had.
Genesis 2:16-17

This was God's first man with a childish heart,
and like a child was easy to deceive.
He had not yet been exposed to sin
and didn't know exactly what to believe.
Genesis 3:6

Ah, but you know better, for you have been taught,
and you have a better covenant today.
God has placed His law in your heart and mind;
childish things should have been put away.
Hebrew 10:16-17   Jeremiah 31:33-34
I Corinthians 13:11

The garden of Eden and the heart of man,
the places where God make things grow,
are really the same in the spirit realm;
read the word to understand and to know.
II Corinthians13:5   Proverbs 4:7

In each of these gardens, someone is in charge,
to care for, to nurture, to tend.
If either are neglected, they will be overcome,
grown over with thorns or with sin.
Proverbs 24:30-34

I refer to Adam and the Holy Spirit
as the leader, the teacher, the guide.
In the garden of Eden or the garden of your heart,
God is at both of their sides.
John 14:6   Hebrews 13:5

God is looking for someone to make up the hedge,
to stand in the gap for the land.
He made us all after His likeness;
we are His portraits of a man.
Ezekiel 22:30

He is our shepherd, we are his flock,
we are the sheep of his pasture you know.
A shepherd does not increase his flock,
it's the sheep who reproduce and make it grow.
Ezekiel 34:31

TRIVIAL PURSUIT

Our attitude toward spiritual death determines
how we physically live or whether we go off on a
TRIVIAL PURSUIT
The hunt for, the chase of, or the effort to secure
something insignificant or of very little importance.

Men who seek for earthly treasures,
Think little about the thief.
They lay up riches for themselves,
while causing harm and grief.
Matthew 6:19-21
Luke 12:21

They think not much about the moth,
or the corrupting nature of rust.
The money they have is clearly inscribed,
bold letters, "In God We Trust."
Matthew 19:21
Luke 12:33

The things of the world tug at man's heart;
these things have a very high price.
We should lay up treasures for ourselves in heaven,
because our richness comes through Christ.
Matthew 6:20

Not the lust of the flesh, nor the lust of the eyes,
and not through the pride of life —
These things of the world will pass away,
and they all bring misery and strife.
I John 2:15-17

Only those things that we do for God
will provide that salvation link.
Every way of a man is right to himself,
but God's record is in **ETERNAL INK.**
Proverbs 21:2

Man looketh on the outward appearance;
the Lord pondereth the heart for wealth.
There is a way that seems right to a man,
but the ends thereof are death.
Proverbs 14:12

If you seek first the kingdom of God
and take no thought for the morrow.
All these things shall be added unto you,
and be sufficient till the day of sorrows.
Matthew 6:33-34
Daniel 12:1

The spirit has begun a good work in you,
so be confident of this very thing.
He will perform it until the day of Christ,
when all the heavenly host will sing.
Philippians 1:6   Revelations 19:1-7

Now let's get down to the crux of the matter;
the earth's treasure is no more than rubble;
man born of a woman is of just a few days,
and those days will be full of trouble.
Job 14:1

You must beware lest you be spoiled,
through philosophy and vain deceit.
After traditions of men, after rudiments of the world,
you should lay it all at God's feet.
Colossians 2:8

In the midst of a crooked and perverse nation,
you are to shine as a light in the world.
Being blameless and harmless a son of God,
not caught up in the turmoil and swirl.
Philippians 2:15

Do all things without murmuring and disputing,
for it is God which worketh in you.
Submit to His will by being obedient,
and of His good pleasures do.
Philippians 2:13-14

If we then be risen with Christ
and seek those things above,
The Lord will teach us to number our days,
as we apply our hearts unto love.
Colossians 3:1-4
Psalm 90:12

We cannot just conform to this world
and do our alms before men.
We must prove what is good, acceptable and perfect,
by renewing our minds, turn from sin.
Romans 12:2   Matthew 6:1

Finally, my brethren, be strong in the Lord,
and in the power of His might.
Take unto you the whole armor of God,
because things are going to start to get tight.
Ephesians 6:10-13

Now that you've committed your life to Christ,
Satan is going to be on your trail.
His purpose is to steal your testimony
and to gloat as he watches you fail.
Revelation 12:11

What Satan doesn't know, or understand,
that while he's tempting man with sin,
it has been revealed through the word of God,
if we endure unto the end we win.
Matthew 24:13-14
James 1:12

So no matter what the situation is,
rest assured the devil is near,
trying to snatch God's word to use against you;
those who have ears let him hear.
Mark 4:3-20

The merchandise of gold and precious stones
and all the great cities possess
Will be thrown down and be found no more,
because man has used it all to excess.
Revelation 18:12-21

They were meant for our good, these things we have;
we failed to give God the glory.
We get caught up in pride, lose all self control,
and we don't truly believe **HIS-STORY.**
Romans 8:28   Proverbs 3:6

If you are prospecting for earthly treasure,
spend some time with our Lord and sup.
Unless you're connected with Him, which is life,
you will soon become **SPIRITUALLY BANKRUPT.**
John 15:1-10

And unless you have something to give,
don't expect anyone to ask.
Silver and gold you may not have
but that was not your assigned task
Acts 3:6   Mark 16:15   Acts 20:35

You cannot give what you do not have;
I am referring to Christ and His love.
He is your life, all else is trivial;
store your treasures with Him above.
John 14:6
I Timothy 6:19

Don't be in pursuit of things of this world;
you need the fruit of the Spirit to cope.
You are a man most miserable, according to the Word,
if only in this life you have hope.
Galatians 5:22-23
I Corinthians 15:19

FEAR

I know I am not innocent,
but you are holding me so.
You gave your life that I may live,
and you only bid me go.

Go into all the world and preach,
be instant in season and out.
The foolish and unlearned questions avoid;
trust the Lord with your heart, don't doubt.
II Timothy 4:2   II Timothy 2: 23

The fear of the Lord is the beginning of wisdom;
seek Him whenever you can.
Fear God and keep His commandments;
this is the whole duty of man.
Psalm 111:10   Ecclesiastes 12:13

To depart from evil is understanding;
you can learn this by studying His word.
But to serve our God takes some action;
it's not based on just something you heard.
Job 28:28

The Lord is our light and salvation;
He is the strength of our life.
Whom shall we fear or be afraid?
He knows all of our misery and strife.
Psalm 27:1

God hath not given us the spirit of fear,
but of power, and of love, a sound mind.
Though in the valley of the shadow of death,
He is with you, fear not, be not blind.
II Timothy 1:7   Psalm 23:4   Isaiah 41:10

If when a fear comes upon you,
remember the Lord at your side.
Fear not what man can do unto you,
because in our Lord's love you abide.
Job 34:25
Psalm 118:6

His perfect love casteth out fear;
there is no fear in love.
Fear hath torment, which is not of God;
stay focused on those things above.
I John 4:18

Eye hath not seen, nor hath ear heard,
neither entered into the heart of man,
The things God prepared for those that love him,
we do not as yet understand.
I Corinthians 2:9-12

IT IS DONE

I am the Alpha and Omega, the beginning and the end;
this is what was said to John,
In the book of Revelations, twenty one, six,
when He said unto him, "It is done."
Revelation 21:6

He that was seated upon the throne
is the one who spoke to John.
The Bible I use, Christ's words are in red,
not so, when was spoken, "It Is Done."

What did he mean? Why say that here?
Were these words only for John?
He said put them in writing, they are true and faithful;
what did he mean, "It is done"?
Revelation 21:5-6

This is not the first time we hear these words;
"It is finished" was uttered in pain
By Jesus at Calvary on the Cross of Redemption,
when He gave his life for our gain.
John 19:30

He had finished the work he was given to do;
He had glorified His Father on earth.
He submitted His will and was a living testimony,
who never changed from the day of his birth.
John 17:4

His purpose was to reconcile us back to God;
this is really why he was sent,
to seek and to save those that are lost,
and to give us a chance to repent.
Isaiah 61:1-2   Luke 4:18-19   II Corinthians 5:18-21

He was sent as a Lamb among the wolves,
and he knew what he had to do;
to fulfill the word meant giving his life,
and that was done for me and for you.
Matthew 10:16
Matthew 5:17

If and whenever you are given a mission
and you've completed the task at hand,
you still have to do the paperwork
and make a final report to the man.
Revelation 20:12

Whoever sent you to do the job
is the one you should look to for pay.
He is the one that gives the instructions
and the only one you should obey.
John 4:34

When you finish the work you are given to do,
it looks good on the entire team.
It shows we are fitly joined together
and have all things in common it seems.
John 17:4

It shows we are one and that we agree,
but we have different jobs to do.
Our common theme, the point of our being,
is to help the Old Man become New.
Ephesians 4:22-32

In order to help our fellow man,
we must each first examine ourself.
We cannot give what we do not have,
have we been the victim of theft?
II Corinthians 13:5   John 10:10

I believe when He said "It is done,"
that he meant all things are made new.
He had fulfilled his purpose and made his report,
the rest is up to me and to you.
Revelations 21:6

He spoke of things present and of things past
and was speaking of things to come;
His earthly ministry, His heavenly ministry,
all of it now had been done.

It was done when He spoke it, it simply became,
just like He had done before.
He spoke things into existence
from Genesis to Revelations,
a fact that no man can ignore.

He had overcome all of earth's obstacles;
all essence of His ministry was done.
He was now back in heaven with His Father;
on the throne they again were one.

They were always one in the spirit realm,
but there was a time of separation.
The Word became flesh and took on sin;
it was for us He was making preparations

We too must overcome in order to inherit;
we each must endure till the end.
We're new creatures in Christ, He did his part;
It's up to us to live a life free of sin.
Revelations 21:7   Mark 13:13
II Corinthians 5:17

We are joint heirs with Christ,
we have the same ministry,
but to reign we must also suffer.
He abides in our heart, gives new mercy each day,
and the Holy Spirit is our buffer.

The race is not given to the swift,
nor the battle to the strong.
Be about your Father's business,
"It Is Done," "It Is Done," as your song.

THIS PRECIOUS GIFT

Do you want what God has for you?
It will give your life a lift.
If you say yes to the word you heard,
you can receive this precious gift.
Deuteronomy 30:15, 19
Joshua 24:15

It may not be wrapped the way you want,
and not tied with a big red bow,
but your Father sent it and He knows best;
it's what's inside that counts, you know.
John 3:17
John 5:37-38

If you knew the gift of God
and who it is who says to you:
"Give me to drink," you would have asked Him
for living water, springing up, making new.
John 4:10-14

What He is giving is all of himself;
in your heart He wants to abide.
To accept this gift I must be quite frank;
there are some things you must lay aside.
John 15:4-7
Hebrew 12:1

Things may not happen just all of a sudden;
there may be no great blinding light.
This gift of love may be revealed to you
in a calm still voice at night.
I Kings 19:1-12
Acts 9:1-5

How ever it's delivered, the gift is the same;
it arrives when your life's in a mess.
It does not always lift us from trouble;
it's a process, there will be a test.
Isaiah 55:8-9, 11

You are required to repent and be baptized
in the name of Jesus Christ for your sin.
You shall receive the gift, the Holy Spirit,
and your new life with God will begin.
Acts 2:38

Even though God has this gift for you,
and He has offered to you His best,
the gift is still His until you accept
and enter into His rest.
Hebrew 4:1-6

Accepting the gift begins a new life,
so it's open, now what do you do.
Begin to use what you just received;
share with others like God did with you.

You were not forced to receive God's gift,
so don't try to force it on others.
Let your speech be seasoned with salt;
know how to answer your brothers.
Colossians 4:6
I Peter 3:15

Meet them where they are, on their level;
let the Holy Spirit flow anew.
Impart to them the Gospel of Christ,
from the Spirit of love within you.
Mark 16:15

You cannot be filled with the Holy Spirit
until you yield yourself to the Lord.
This precious gift being offered to you
is for free, you just ask, it's not hard.
Acts 8:14-20

As it is written in the word of the Lord,
man can baptize you with water.
You need the baptism that comes only from God,
this precious gift, the Holy Spirit, from your Father.
Acts 1:5
Acts 11:15-17

BOUGHT WITH A PRICE

The weight of the world is not on our shoulders;
we're in sin because we want to be.
We were bought with a price, our Lord gave His life
when He died so we could be free.
Isaiah 9:6
I Corinthians 6:20 and 7:23

For our light afflictions, which is but for a moment,
is working eternal weight in glory.
We cast our cares upon Christ our Lord,
but we don't yet understand **His Story.**
II Corinthians 4:17
I Peter 5:7

Remember ye not the former things,
neither consider the things of old.
We were not redeemed with corruptible things;
it was the blood of Christ, not gold.
Isaiah 43:18-19
I Peter 1:18-19

What we don't know we can't relate;
we must have before we can give.
The things of old must pass away;
we must die before we can live.
Hosea 4:6   John 12:24-25
II Corinthians 5:17

Since we are surrounded by a cloud of witnesses
and our endurance determines our fate,
Those things that ensnare or so easily beset,
let them go, lay aside, sin and weight.
Hebrews 12:1
Matthew 24:13

It is time for us to count up the cost,
but I can only speak for me.
I was bought with a price, Christ gave His life;
I can't act like salvation is free.
Luke 14:28   Romans 5:8-9

It's free to us, it's a **Precious Gift,**
but Christ our Lord had to pay.
In reverence to Him and all that he's done,
we can't act just any kind of way.
Galatians 5:1
Romans 5:15-19

We are his ambassadors and must represent him,
remember we were made in his image.
We are joint heirs with Christ, Who gave his life
and fulfilled our spiritual lineage.
Genesis 1:26
Galatians 4:7
Romans 8:16-17

God does not expect us to die on the cross,
but our cross is ours to carry.
We each have a ministry to complete,
and tomorrow is not promised, don't tarry.
Luke 14:27
Mark 10:21
Matthew 25:13

We each have a price to pay;
some may have more than others.
What are you doing with what you have?
Is it helping your neighbors and brothers?
Matthew 25:14-28

What brings Him glory? What brings Him honor?
What would He have us to do?
Accept His gift, then share it with others;
help make old things become new.

Go ye into all the world and preach;
live a righteous and holy lifestyle.
Love your neighbor as you love yourself,
and for them always go the last mile.
Matthew 19:19
Luke 10:30-37

THE MARRIAGE / WEDDING FEAST

You have been invited to the wedding,
do you have some other plan?
Dinner is prepared, all things are ready;
people are bidden throughout the land.
Matthew 22:2-4

Don't make light of this wedding feast,
it's an honor to be a guest.
Those asked first that would not come
were destroyed, cities burned, what a mess.
Matthew 22:5-8

The host of this great marriage feast
is doing this for his best.
Make sure you're present on the wedding day,
and have on the proper dress.
Matthew 22:2, 11-13

You must be adorned inside and out;
your heart and lifestyle must attest
that you are present at this marriage feast,
in the garment of righteousness.

Man looketh on the outward appearance,
but God looketh on the heart with pride.
You are not just an invited guest;
prepare yourself to be the bride.
Revelation 21:2

John was allowed to see the Lamb's wife,
clothed in the garment of salvation,
Observing and doing whatsoever He commanded,
an oiled vessel, teaching all nations.
Isaiah 61:10
Matthew 25:10   Matthew 28:20

The bride will be the one that has overcome
tribulations and endured to the end.
Though suffering afflictions, the bride keeps the faith,
she has the promise of the groom, she will win.
Matthew 24:13

Blessed art thou among the people;
your changed heart has made you new.
You are the temple of the Holy Ghost,
now that Spirit resides in you.
Luke 1:42

At this wedding feast we all become one;
this is where the glories meet.
It's the new heaven and the new earth,
all things are now under our feet.
Revelation 21:1, 23-26

Satan has been defeated, his strongholds destroyed;
eternal life will be glorious and simple,
blessings, glory, thanksgiving, honor,
serving God night and day in His temple.
Revelation 7: 12

HEART, MIND, SOUL

The heart of man is the battleground;
that's where God's law is encased.
Our heart is what the devil wants;
God's goodness he wants to replace.
Jeremiah 31:33

The mind of man, another battlefield,
old Satan comes with a thought.
It's up to us to entertain it or not,
but the mind is where it's fought.
Hebrew 10:16

The soul of man is the ultimate goal;
there is a purpose for our living,
To glorify God and enjoy Him forever;
it began with Jesus' giving.
Matthew 10:28
Luke 9:24

He gave his life to set us free,
so the battle is already won.
Revere God now and keep His commandments;
we're just another prodigal son.
Luke 15:11-24
Ecclesiastes 12:13

We go our own way and do our own thing;
a lot of youthful years are spent
in the world of sin and self-gratification;
we are given the time to repent.
Luke 15:12-16

When we come to ourself and see where we are
and we realize we have a Father,
Our goods have been wasted, we want to come home,
but we don't want to be a bother.
Luke 15:17-19

Our Father will welcome us with open arms;
He has saved for us His best.
He always loved us in spite of ourselves;
we just had to pass some test
Luke 15:20-23

There is joy in the presence of the Angels above
over one sinner that repents.
The illustration of the prodigal son
details how our lives are spent.
Luke 14:10

Christian character is being developed
all the while we are going through.
It's a part of God's plan, it's a process
our spirits to renew.

We don't suddenly arrive, just overnight,
our faith grows day by day.
You see the devil believes, just like you,
but he refuses to obey.

And he is who our battle is with,
spiritual wickedness in high places.
The sooner we define the battlefield,
we'll start to see his many faces.

TEACH

To make known in a sermon, to give earnest advice,
that's what we do when we preach.
The congregation, however, sometimes has questions,
and the servant must be apt to teach.
II Timothy 2:24

All scripture is given by inspiration of God,
of the five-fold ministry take heed
Apostle, prophet, evangelist, pastor
and the teacher, Christian families need.
II Timothy 3:16
Colossians 4:17
Ephesians 4:11

My son, be strong in the grace that's in Christ
and the things thou hast heard of me;
the same commit thou to faithful men
who shall teach like it was taught to thee.
II Timothy 2:1-2

Study to show thyself approved
and rightly divide the Word;
shun vain babblings and shun the profane,
you can't teach everything you heard.
II Timothy 2:15-16

Speak thou the things which become sound doctrine;
observe the things I have commanded you.
I am with you always, unto the end of the world
in the Old Testament and the New.
Titus 2:1
Matthew 28:20

Go ye therefore and teach all nations
in this present world how we should live,
and as you stand, proclaiming God's word,
teach them also to forgive.
Matthew 18:35, 28:19
Titus 2:12
Mark 11:26

Train up a child in the way he should go;
bend them during youth toward the light.
When he is old, he'll not depart from it;
it's hard to bind the strong man in his might.
Proverbs 22:6
Judges 16:1-31

Teach every man to be swift to hear,
but slow to wrath and to speak.
You can gain the whole world and still lose your soul;
it's the kingdom of God man should seek.
James 1:19
Matthew 6:33 and 16:26

Teach man about the tree of life
in the midst of New Jerusalem street,
whose leaf shall be for healing the nations
and the fruit thereof for meat.
Ezekiel 47:12
Revelation 22:2

The fruit of the Spirit and the character of Christ
teach man that they are the same;
the fruit of love embodies them all,
and this is why Christ came.
Galatians 5:22
Ephesians 5:9
I John 4:8

That he might destroy the works of the devil,
for this purpose he was manifested.
He completed his mission through love and obedience;
now each one of us must be tested.
I John 3:8

He's the example of what we should teach;
closely study the book of John.
As a child of God, strive to be one with him,
just like he and his Father are one.
John Chapter 2-10

HUMAN CHARACTER TRAITS

INTEGRITY: Moral soundness, dependability, honesty, loyalty, courageous, consistent, the ability to keep your word.

SENSE OF RESPONSIBILITY: The driving or motivating force within a person that gives them the awareness to recognize and do what must be done. Staying with the job until the job is complete. Accepting all assignments.

HUMANENESS: Show a sincere regard for others, treat people like people. Understanding of human behavior to recognize basic needs and desires.

ENTHUSIASM: This is a quality that is transferred to others. Interest and sincerity generate enthusiasm, which results in diligence, perseverance and aggressiveness — excitement.

EMOTIONAL STABILITY: This is expressed basically in self control. Emotions should not interfere with what you have to do — patience, temperament.

PROFESSIONAL COMPETENCE: Know your job. Make every effort to keep your knowledge current. Study and talk to others to prepare yourself to do a better job.

SELF CONFIDENCE: The inner strength that enables you to overcome obstacles. Freedom from doubt. Believe in yourself.

TACT: Saying the kindest and most fitting things, skill in dealing with others. Considerate.

PRINCIPLES OF
LEADERSHIP / DISCIPLESHIP

1. Know your job

2. Know yourself and seek improvements

3. Know your people and look out for their welfare

4. Keep your people informed

5. Set the example

6. Train your people as a team

7. Seek responsibility and develop a sense of responsibility in your people

8. Make sound timely decisions

9. Be sure the task is understood, supervised and accomplished.

CHRISTIAN CHARACTER EXAMPLES IN THE BOOK OF JOHN

Chapter

2:14-16   Is courageous, willing to confront
the establishment when it is in the wrong.

2:23-25   Understands human behavior.

3:1-2   Is available day and night.

3:17   Committed to improvement.

4:7-10   Willing to talk to others,
provides encouragement.

5:30,41   Seeks God's approval for what he does
(God is the supreme authority, not man).

6:10-12   Is well organized, uses subordinates,
gives orders, maintains order.

6:18-21   Remains calm in time of crisis,
goes to his people when they are in need.

7:7   Points out wrong.

7:18   Brings glory to the one represented,
not oneself.

7:24   Thinks through each situation
and encourages others to think.

8:2   Is early on the scene, eager to talk and teach.

8:10-11   Forgives but corrects the error.

9:39   Clarifies misunderstandings.

10:11   Subjugates his will to the will / needs of his
        people.

10:14   Knows his people; his people know him.

THE FRUIT OF THE SPIRIT
Will Produce the Christian Character in Us

Love Devotion, affection, the fulfilling of the law. Who God is.

Joy Source and provider of happiness or pleasure.

Peace Without stress or anxiety, harmony.

Patience Uncomplaining, long-suffering.

Kindness Warm-hearted, forgiving, considerate, humane.

Goodness Moral excellence, admirable.

Faithfulness Complete confidence.

Gentleness Mild, mellow wisdom, pleasing.

Self Control Able to remain calm in a crisis.

Righteousness Adhering to moral principles.

Truth Verified facts.

Obedience Willing submissive behavior.

THE FRUIT OF THE TREE OF LIFE
Will Sustain the Christian Character in Us

Obedience   Willing, submissive behavior.

Grace   God's unmerited favor.

Faith   Complete confidence, trust, reliance and belief.

Salvation   Rescue, deliverance, preservation.

Choice   Options.

Repentance   Change, regret, turning.

Wisdom   True and right discernment.

Integrity   Uprightness of character.

Righteousness Virtuous, adhering to moral principles.

Redemption   Recovery.

Seed   Word.

Living Word   Jesus.

THE FRUIT OF OBEDIENCE

God provided Adam and Eve the fruit of **Obedience.** As long as they ate of that fruit, their lives were sustained. The fruit of obedience produced within Adam and Eve **eternal life.** Their disobedience produced death, physical as well as spiritual. *Gen. 2:16-17, Romans 5:12-20.*

God provided Noah the fruit of **Grace.** *Gen. 6:8.* The fruit of grace produced a **remnant** in the earth. *Gen. 8:20-22.*

God provided Abraham the fruit of **Faith,** *Gen. 12:1-3,* which in turn produced a **covenant.** *Gen. 22:1-18.*

God provided Moses the fruit of **Salvation.** *Exodus 3:9-10; 12:12-14; 14:13-14.* The fruit of salvation produced **freedom.** *Exodus 14:26-31.*

God provided Joshua the fruit of **choice.** *Deut. 30:1-20, Joshua 1:1-9.* The fruit of choice produced **fellowship.** *Joshua 24:1-28.*

God provided David the fruit of **repentance.** *II Samuel 12:1-12; 24:1-15.* The fruit of repentance produced **forgiveness.** *II Samuel 12:13-14; 24:17.*

God provided Solomon the fruit of **wisdom.** *I Kings 3:10-14.* The fruit of wisdom produced an **understanding heart.** *I Kings 3:1-9.*

God provided Job the fruit of **integrity.** *Job 1:1, 7:22 and 2:1-6.* The fruit of integrity produced **glory.** *Job 42:10, chapters 38, 39, 40:1-2.*

God provided Isaiah the fruit of **righteousness.** *Isa. 6:1-13.* The fruit of righteousness produced a **garment.** *Job 29:14; Isa. 11:5, 59:17, 61:10, and Rev. 19:8.*

God provided Hosea the fruit of **redemption.** *Hosea 1:2-11, 2:1-5.* The fruit of redemption produced a **ransom,** *Hosea 3:1-5; Isaiah 53:10-12,* and **restoration.** *Isaiah 53:1-9.*

God provided Mary the **seed** of the Living Word, *Luke 1:26-37,* which was **conceived** in her, *Luke 1:35, 38,* and was birthed as the **son of the living God — Jesus Christ.** *Matt. 1:21-23.*

God provided the world **his only begotten son,** *John 3:16,* who in turn sent the **Holy Spirit** and the fruit thereof. *Galatians 5:22, Ephesians 5:9.*

Jesus Christ — God incarnate (embodied in flesh or human form) is the **obedience, grace, faith, salvation, choice, repentance, wisdom, integrity, righteousness, redemption, seed, living word, love, joy, peace, patience, kindness, goodness, gentleness, self-control** and **truth** we need to help us **"Rise Above It All."**

FLOWERS

As beautiful as these flowers are,
Not all of them started from seed.
They were placed in this very room
because there was a need.

As you take time to admire their beauty,
may they remind you of yourself.
A withering, dying, pitiful person
now thriving on God's shelf.

He placed you in His vase of love;
His mercy and grace you were fed.
You are now well-rooted and grounded
and ready to be led.

Grow toward the light just like these plants
because you are someone's flower.
They see in you a source of strength,
of beauty, of love, a tower.

They may not always understand
how to water, care and do,
but you are still their flower,
and they see the beauty in you.

ABOUT THE AUTHOR

Hervey L. Chambers is the son of the late L.B. And Trusilar Chambers of Cleveland, Arkansas (Center Community).

He is an Ordained Deacon, a retired United States Air Force Master Sergeant and former Director of Education for the 22nd Air Force Noncommissioned Officers Leadership School at Little Rock Air Force Base.

Currently, Hervey is the Security Supervisor of the Court Security Officers at the United States Bankruptcy Court in Little Rock, Arkansas. He is a Special Deputy, United States Marshal with the Court Security Division, and is responsible for the protection of the Federal Judiciary and Staff assigned in the Eastern District of Arkansas. He also performs other duties as directed by the U.S. Marshal, U.S. Magistrates or the Federal Judges.

Hervey resides in Jacksonville, Arkansas. He and his late wife, Jennifer K. (Smith) Chambers, have three children, Leslie, Mallory and LaKesha.

They have six grandchildren: Anthony, Andre, Jaida, Ariana, Christian and Elijah.

HERVEY L. CHAMBERS
completes his third book!

"Son Rise," "A Walk With The Son" and **"Rise Above It All"** are collections of inspirational poetry complete with scriptural verses. Each poem bears its own message, while contributing to the total message relayed on the title pages.

To order copies complete the information below.

Ship to: *(please print)*

Name:_____

Address:_____

City, State:_____Zip_____

Day Phone:_____Business Phone_____

___Copies of **"Son Rise"** .... @ $12.00 each $_____

___Copies of **"A Walk With The Son"** @ $12.00 each $_____

___Copies of **"Rise Above It All"** ...... @ $12.00 each $_____

    Postage and Handling .... @ $2.50/book $_____

    Overseas .... @ $4.50/book $_____

    Arkansas Resident Sales Tax .... $_____

    Total Amount Enclosed .... $_____

Arkansas sales tax does not apply to out-of-state residents.

Make cashier's checks or money orders payable to:
        Hervey L. Chambers
Mail to: P.O. Box # 6201
        Jacksonville, Arkansas 72076-5741

http://MyWebPages.comcast.net/hchambers8/
hchambers8@comcast.net
1-501-517-4794